Unleashing the Power c

Unleashing the Power of Diversity provides a clear tool to create a common language across teams and organisations that reinforces positive identity, builds trust towards people and processes, supports innovation and helps make diversity sustainable.

The complex problems that many organisations and teams now face are global in scope, including cultural, social and environmental issues. Challenges such as climate change, mass migration and human rights do not respect national borders or sociodemographic groups. In order to solve these complex problems, we need the skills to be able to communicate effectively across the differences that may otherwise divide us.

In this ground-breaking book, award-winning consultant and author, Bjørn Z. Ekelund, presents a clear step-by-step approach to communicate with people who have different mindsets, perspectives and cultural backgrounds. It is relevant and applicable across various contexts – within the workplace, inter-professional, across different industries and cultures, and between corporate, governmental and NGO groups.

The program developed in the book, called the Diversity Icebreaker, has been successfully applied across 70 countries and with 250,000 participants. It shows how to break down these barriers and provides a new way to conceptualise diversity across various boundaries, allowing for trust and unity to form and creating a pathway for improving communication.

Bjørn Z. Ekelund is Senior Consultant and Chairman of the Board at Human Factors AS, Norway, and Research Fellow at the Centre for Global Workforce Strategy, Simon Fraser University, Canada.

"It is our pleasure to endorse Bjørn Ekelund and his new book and it comes with our best recommendation. In RETHNK we design and facilitate strategic change and we create spectacular transformative workshops. We use the Diversity Icebreaker concept to improve communication and understanding between participants during a workshop. Advanced workshop facilitation brings people through three stages in our accelerated workshop: Learn, Integrate and Transform, which is also represented as a Green, Red and Blue process. The feedback we get from our customers is great because the Diversity Icebreaker helps them communicate in a simple way about complex problems."

Jesper Sonne and Carsten Arnfjord Thomsen, RETHNK, Denmark

"I have been using the Diversity Icebreaker for over 10 years with executives, graduate students and undergraduates. The class sizes have ranged from 11 to 60 participants. It has become an important tool in my courses for under-standing diversity in patterns of interpersonal behavior, communication styles and work preferences. Although there is substantial statistical data for its relia-bility and validity, I find its face validity, simple (but not simplistic) categoriza-tion scheme and ease of use to be critical characteristics. I am not trying to make my students pop psychologists but rather provide a tool to help them to become more effective. Participants clearly recognize the three styles in their organizations and find that it usually identifies their style accurately. In addition to learning, they really enjoy the exercise."

Dr. Henry Lane, D'Amore-McKim School of Business, Northeastern University, Boston, MA

"One of the main difficulties working in collaborative processes where mutual respect and equality among participants are core values is the lack of a common language. Especially in welfare programs where so-called clients or other end-users of public service are invited into processes where empowerment and governance are explicit goals. Even with such aims, the dialogue often seems to move into forms and meaning that support one side, and that is seldom the most vulnerable ones. The Diversity Icebreaker does not take into account who has most prestige or which prior position the participant has in front of a DI working session. A DI session is instead coloured in a playful atmosphere where the participants gather around new concepts; Red, Green and Blue with a dialogue spinning out of those concepts with very few predefined influences from any given positions."

Lars Ueland Kobro, CEO/Senior researcher, Norwegian Centre for Social Entrepre-neurship and Social Innovation – SESAM, University of South-Eastern Norway

."Self-understanding, understanding the Other, acknowledgement, belonging, inclusiveness, trust, common language, team work and … fun. So many leit-motifs that run through the book and reflect our experience of using the Diversity Icebreaker with all the staff and students at our school for the last five years. Through the hundreds of sessions we have run with staff and students from over 100 countries, we have come to rely on the Diversity Icebreaker as one of the basic tools in our intercultural communication toolbox."

Grant Douglas, Track Coordinator, Intercultural Communication, IESEG School of Management, Lille, France

"I have been fortunate to work with Bjørn Z. Ekelund and the Diversity Icebreaker for more than 10 years. I have found him and the use of Diversity Icebreaker to be under constant development. Bjørn is engaging and a true knowledge sharer, making the research-based tool, the Diversity Icebreaker, easy to use for mentoring large groups of up to 150 participants. The Diversity Icebreaker is always highly appreciated and has received excellent feedback from leaders and employees around the world."

Annika Dybwad, Owner and senior consultant, FlexAbility Consulting AS, Norway

"I have had the pleasure of using the Diversity Icebreaker in diverse learning settings, including courses in Design Thinking and Action Research. In these courses, the Diversity Icebreaker created a powerful vehicle for deep learning at multiple levels. This includes learning about self in relation to others in the context of collaborative projects that value multiple perspectives, fostering systemic understanding in working with wicked problems."

Frederick Steier, Ph.D., Professor, Fielding Graduate University, School of Leadership Studies, and Department of Communication, University of South Florida

Unleashing the Power of Diversity
How to Open Minds for Good

Bjørn Z. Ekelund

Routledge
Taylor & Francis Group

LONDON AND NEW YORK

First published 2019
by Routledge
2 Park Square, Milton Park, Abingdon, Oxon OX14 4RN

and by Routledge
52 Vanderbilt Avenue, New York, NY 10017

Routledge is an imprint of the Taylor & Francis Group, an informa business

British Library Cataloguing-in-Publication Data
A catalogue record for this book is available from the British Library

Library of Congress Cataloging-in-Publication Data
Names: Ekelund, Bjørn Z., author.
Title: Unleashing the power of diversity : how to open minds for
good / Bjørn Z. Ekelund.
Description: Abingdon, Oxon ; New York, NY : Routledge, 2019. |
Includes bibliographical references and index.
Identifiers: LCCN 2019003213| ISBN 9781138602700 (hardback) |
ISBN 9781138602717 (pbk.) | ISBN 9780429469466 (ebook)
Subjects: LCSH: Diversity in the workplace. | Intercultural
communication. | Multiculturalism.
Classification: LCC HF5549.5.M5 E44 2019 | DDC 658.3008--dc23
LC record available at https://lccn.loc.gov/2019003213

ISBN: 978-1-138-60270-0 (hbk)
ISBN: 978-1-138-60271-7 (pbk)
ISBN: 978-0-429-46946-6 (ebk)

Typeset in Bembo
by Taylor & Francis Books

Contents

Illustrations

Figures

Cases

Acknowledgements

The concept of Diversity Icebreaker starts in 1994 when I was invited to take part in solving a wicked problem with a client. The invitation came from my marketing colleagues in a co-working space in Tønsberg in Norway. Since then, there have been more than 50 people who have been working with me directly and contributed in different ways to the development of the concept. I am a very "Green" person, and in my case that seems to express as being dedicated, challenging, professionally proud, creative and stubborn. These are qualities that probably have not made me the most easy-going person to work with. But, I hope that the generosity, openness and willingness to share and democratize knowledge has compensated for some of these other qualities.

I want to give my thanks especially to those who more than others have been central in different stages of the development of Diversity Icebreaker/ Red, Blue and Green since 1994: To Sven-Tore Jensen and Bjørn Hesthag: In 1994, you initiated the search for new communication strategies for the Akershus Energy conservation department, giving me the commercial opportunity to develop Red, Blue and Green by helping engineers to reduce energy consumption through lots of different initiatives during the last part of the 1990s.

Terje Øveraas and Tom Grankel: Thanks for inviting me into an inter-disciplinary project that focused on solving the client challenge from Akershus Energy conservation department in 1994.

Jon Lambrechts: You and I formed the company Human Factors AS in Oslo in 1996 and together we defined our business values and practice in developing our company in the creative space between academic vs practical and analysis vs development. The development of Diversity Icebreaker into a unique seminar is a consequence of this platform. The values still inspire.

Martha L Maznevski: In 1997 we met and you introduced me to a globally oriented academic network that later was organised and named, International Organisation Network. My global experience and worldview and my confidence as a relevant contributor in this field would not have happened without your invitation to take part in this network.

Christine and Adrian Atkinson. You motivated me to finish my MBA dissertation in 1997 at Henley Management College where I documented the success of the application of Red, Blue and Green to reduce energy. Your proofreading of the dissertation was your gift to me when I celebrated my 40 years anniversary.

Trond Ivar Hegge: In 1997, you were doing the first reliability analysis of the Diversity Icebreaker questionnaire and contributed to the different analysis of Red, Blue and Green in different market segments.

Kari Jørstad: You co-developed the first seminar practices with me and co-authored our first team training book for facilitators where Red, Blue and Green was presented in 2000.

Joy Buikema Fjærtoft: You were the one that systematically developed training material and seminar practices with me in the years after 2000.

Michel Esnault: In 2008, you co-authored a book on project start-ups with me where the human side of managing diversity was included and through your own practice, brought the Diversity Icebreaker experience into the project management field.

Eva Langvik: You co-edited and authored the first research volume on Diversity Icebreaker with me in 2008 and contributed your knowledge of methods and analysis that made us move forward in the academic practice.

Sue Canney Davison: You were the first to formulate advanced training material for Red, Blue and Green global use with me in 2002 and who, through your international experience, validated my ideas at that time for a global practice. You also helped me in writing this book as an English speaking editor, helping with the language and fluency of ideas throughout the book.

Living as a full time consultant and at the same time pushing research based development is a challenge without good cooperation with others closer to the academic field. Since 2004 these people have jointly been working with me in the development of Diversity Icebreaker. We have together presented at professional and academic conferences and written articles, chapters and books together. Without this network of contributors it would not have been possible to develop a globally relevant and research based concept: Eva Langvik, Linn Slettum Bjerke, Teresa J. Rothausen-Vange, Rotem Shneor, Bettina Gerke, Miriam Nordgård, Martha L. Maznevski, Joe DiStefano, Leah Davcheva, Jan Viggo Iversen, Torill Moe, Kazuma Matoba, Alexis Rossi, Marieke Van Egmond, Laurence Romani, Sue Canney Davison, Solgunn Gjerde, Vivian Boodhun, Ingerid Guttormsgard, Yul Shah Malde, Astrid Handeland, Ole Petter Dahlmann, Kems Adu Gyan, Annika Dybwad, Katherine Johnston, Kristin Fjell, Harry Lane, Roar Samuelsen, Jarle Løvland, Erika Søfting, Monica Sivertsen, Piotr Pluta, Anne-Britt Mokastet Pemzec, Simen M. Ekelund, Ivana Petrović, Lilach Sagiv, Sharon Arieli, Tammy Rubel-Lifschitz, and Andrey Elster.

For the last six years, Human Factors AS has been a group of four people dedicated to Diversity Icebreaker. We have constituted a core group in our network of associated consultants worldwide. The continuity of the organisation since the early 1990s has made it possible to develop the concept as a Norwegian concept with a global outreach. Tanja Münchausen has been managing our customer requests worldwide. Piotr Pluta has been my psychological supporting hand these last seven years. My brother and commercial colleague Harald K. Ekelund has played a unique role, working with me since 1997. He was the one who has pointed out over many years the possibilities of moving the concept from a freely shared one page copy-machine concept to an economically sustainable business. Without his constantly reminding us of this opportunity, we would still be trapped in our first solutions developed in 1998.

I thank all these work colleagues, but even more so, my foundations and strongest gratitude lie embedded within my own family. My two sons, Tarjei Zakarias and Simen Marenius, who in all their years never have experienced a father without a Red, Blue and Green perspective travelling all over the world. And, my deepest thanks go to my wife, Aina Aske, who has given everything of herself to create and nurture our family at home while giving me her unwavering trust and support to follow my vision, ideas and initiatives to work with people all over the world for these last 30 years.

Preface

When people come together from different cultures and scientific backgrounds to solve wicked problems, how can they significantly increase their chances of success? This question has motivated me in my practice as a consultant for the last 30 years. In this book I present the evolution of the most valuable answer I can currently offer.

The ambition is to present the Diversity Icebreaker concept in depth in a way that makes it relevant for doing Good. The concept has gradually evolved since its inception in Norway in 1995. At the time, the concept did not have a strict psychological and theoretical underpinning, but rather grew out of a practical problem-solving exercise. Nevertheless, its growth has been a fascinating non-linear process where surprising experiences have created opportunities for further application, understanding the theoretical basis, developing the product and growing internationally.

The initial challenge was to support engineers to successfully communicate energy saving strategies in such a way that clients would actually adopt them. Having done this, a simple questionnaire was developed as a central element to research and understand how this came about. We positioned the questionnaire as a team role concept in our training of team consultants. Interestingly, the simplicity of the core questionnaire around three distinct categories, Red, Blue and Green, progressed naturally into being able to deepen the power and understanding of the categories in follow on seminars.

As we learnt more, we began to see the global potential for this integration of a questionnaire into a seminar, which in 2005 we named Diversity Ice-breaker. These seminars have become the most satisfactory part of what we can offer. We have also continued to deepen our research within the academic community and elicit the theoretical underpinnings of what we discovered through working with real people in practical situations.

Even though the concept developed from practice, the different theoretical perspectives have fuelled our understanding and continuous improvement. Scientific principles and theories from psychology, sociology, pedagogics, linguistic and social constructivism have been the most pertinent. The therapeutic practice of insight and reflexivity has been inspiring us to deliver the concept to as many people, organisations and communities as possible. More than a quarter of a million people in more than 75 countries have applied the concept so far. This continual growth validates the relevance and practical application of the concept as well as the importance of this book.

I am the person who formed the first ideas of this concept and who has so far remained the most central person in almost 25 years of developing its usefulness. This growth has been anchored in a small consultation company in Norway named Human Factors AS (www.human-factors.no). Global access to the concept is available at www.diversityicebreaker.com.

1 Introduction

Diversity Icebreaker's potential of doing Good

Among the reasons that favoured the outbreak of the conflict is the most banal and ancient one: water. In fact, between 2007 and 2010 Syria was hit by a severe drought, the worst registered in the country over the last century, which left a million small farmers unemployed, and caused the migration of rural populations towards cities. A study published in the journal Proceedings of the National Academy of Sciences, *shows how drought in Syria intensified social uprising, exacerbating the pre-existing political instability.*

According to the team of researchers, the water crisis – caused by decreased winter rainfall and rising temperatures – has probably been worsened by human-driven climate change. "We're not saying the drought caused the war", said Richard Seager, climate scientist at Columbia University's Lamont-Doherty Earth Observatory and co-author of the study. "We're saying that added to all the other stressors, it helped kick things over the threshold into open conflict." (Lifegate, 2018)

Over the past two decades, the global population of forcibly displaced people has grown substantially from 33.9 million in 1997 to 65.6 million in 2016, and it remains at a record high. The growth was concentrated between 2012 and 2015, driven mainly by the Syrian conflict along with other conflicts in the region such as in Iraq and Yemen, as well as in sub-Saharan Africa including Burundi, the Central African Republic, the Democratic Republic of the Congo, South Sudan, and Sudan. (UNHCR, 2016)

An estimated 362,000 refugees and migrants risked their lives crossing the Mediterranean Sea in 2016, with 181,400 people arriving in Italy and 173,450 in Greece. In the first half of 2017, over 105,000 refugees and migrants entered Europe. This movement towards Europe continues to take a devastating toll on human life. Since the beginning of 2017, over 2,700 people are believed to have died or gone missing while crossing the Mediterranean Sea to reach Europe, with reports of many others perishing en route. (UNHCR, 2018)

Current challenges

Since 2015, migrants and refugees have chosen to migrate to Europe from Arabic and African countries. They choose to flee mostly from wars, poverty and political malpractice. Ecological crises caused by fast growing populations, land and forest degradation, climate change and increasing droughts, and limited economic opportunities are initiating migration across and between continents on a scale we have not seen before. The increasing ecological imbalance, fuelled by wasteful material consumption is continuing to create different kinds of crises in the oceans and in many places in the world. Most European countries have experienced a growing right wing populistic attitude with scepticism towards immigration. Escape routes across the Mediterranean Sea have been a deathly endeavour for thousands of people. Refugee camps in the southern part of Europe represent a wall of exclusion preventing these refugees and migrants from taking part in "our inherited" wealth and democratic practices.

All these situations raise important questions. "How can we solve problems together? How can we create high quality inclusive decision making? How can we involve people to create ownership to change? How can we show respect for the individual's contribution?" In many of these processes, we will need people interacting for the common good while addressing important issues. Can we create a practice where the processes and structures inspire people to work together? Can both the inspiring process, as well as the product, be a goal at the same time? Can solving problems together be a method to build dignity and simultaneously create an inclusive community?

There are significant challenges in many aspects of crafting successful interaction between those who come together to address the complex issues mentioned above; competence, arenas, accessibility, power, resources and more. In this book, I will focus upon the communicative interaction between people that have very different basic assumptions about what is important in any interaction. I will name this challenge the meeting between "I and the 'Other'". This is the meeting where I meet another person whose values, preferences, knowledge, ideology, competence are very different from my own. The "Other" represents a group of people that I presume to be different from myself. There is the potential of bringing out the best of each of us into the interaction, learning and problem solving. But, this is not easy for many reasons.

As human beings, for most of the time, we have lived in small groups like families, tribes, clans and small communities with daily survival as the main objective. Knowledge, attitudes and values have been transferred from parents and other close elders through upbringing and enculturation. Our destiny has been to belong to groups where members share goals and values and respect roles and rules (Hariri, 2014; Fukuyama, 2014). Strangers have mostly represented threats. The identification of individuals that did not belong to the tribe, and thus represented this threat, became an integrated part of our intuitive reaction pattern outside our conscious awareness (Casey & Robinson, 2017). Are you an insider or outsider? Are you a friend or a foe? To identify which of the categories to apply when meeting with strangers has been an essential question for survival of the tribe. The historical need has become an integrated response pattern that is kicked off before conscious thinking is evoked. The natural response in meeting with what is seen as threatening strangers is "Fight or Flight". This cognitive script is one of our challenges in meeting with the Others. Can we withhold the natural emotional fear and behavioural response of fight or flight? Can we meet Others with another type of awareness, a feeling of mastery in approaching the stranger? Or, can we reframe Others into people seen as non-threatening, possibly valuable Others?

The questions above emerge out of seeing each human being as being formed by her/his phylogenetic history. As we search for answers that do not follow the "natural" course of history so far, we search for new and productive ways of approaching Others based on ideals for how a good society should cope with contemporary and future challenges. Today's ideals go beyond "fight or flight". We want something different and better than what used to be instinctive. In fact, striving for something better can be seen as a main cultural ambition.

We build cultures on ideals and dreams. Culture and nature are opposites in classical anthropological and cultural theories. As human beings we can formulate ideas about "what-is and what might be". We can make this as opposites, form ideals and dreams, and through social interaction and political institutions build cultures that can solve problems together, including changing nature. Moreover, if we solve problems together with dignity, good communication and continual improvement for everyone – then we start forming the ideal society we all strive for. To live the life we want, while solving important problems together is a way of becoming a good person.

Beyond classical anthropological and cultural theories, man-made culture is also simultaneously seen as a part of nature – a perspective more frequently aligned with indigenous people and the way they live. The fact that in the western world, we seriously discuss whether we are in the time of anthropocene,[1] a time when man changes nature in a way that really will for ever be registered as a significant change in the globe's ecosystemic history, is a phenomena that reminds us of where we belong as human beings. It also reminds us that we have the potential power of self-destruction as a species.

As human beings we can continue as before – or we can create something new. This is one of our cultural challenges today. We have the capacity to raise questions in order to change the developmental trajectory of our society (Hariri, 2015). John Steinbeck in his book *East of Eden* ends the story with reflections about individual choice, referring to the word "Timshel" (Steinbeck, 1952). In the American Standard translation this has been translated as an order, "you must'", which aligns with destiny. In the King James translation of the Bible, it has been translated to "shall", underlining the authority of the church. But, the old Hebraic work is more precisely translated as "might become"/"mayish" – leaving the responsibility for taking this opportunity to all humans themselves.

We have the same challenge today. Do we grasp the opportunity? Do we trust our capability to make a change?

This book focuses on how we understand and promote a successful way of interacting when otherness as an important part of the game. A working title for this book has been *I and the Other* inspired by Martin Büber's *I and Thou*. Büber's book inspires good dialogues between people. In this effective dialogue, I want to introduce the Other person, as not only being an ordinary another person – but for me an Other person where I may sometimes add elements of negativity and prejudgement to the qualities of the group that the Other belongs to. By using the Other concept with a big O, I use the category inspired by Edward Said's *Orientalism*. In this book, the "otherness" is the category used when members of a Western European country encounter people from "Arab" countries and judge them, very often, as not being as advanced as themselves.

Using one's own standards, norms and values as the reference point, means the reference point is usually implicitly and explicitly, consciously or unconsciously self-evaluated as a "gold standard". The Other is not as developed as Western European self-perception, in the cultural context, for example, concerning human rights, women's equity, academic institutions, advanced democracy and other social forms and mores.

At the individual level it often leads to an internal situation where the "Other" is perceived as not as open minded, positive, flexible, literate and many other positive self attributes. So, meeting with the "Other" can have an element of "my being better than you". However, one often quickly discovers that presumptions about another person do not fit the reality of the Other. This situation invites someone to acknowledge and go beyond a potential "put-down" attitude by becoming curious to learn more about the individual Other and eventually revise the ideas of the group that the Other belongs to. The revision is needed because the first ideas are based upon a restricted and sometimes wrong, generalised knowledge and generalisation or stereotype of the Other. The challenge is there because our idea of ourselves being "better than" represents a lack of respect and disrupts effective dialogue. It is a "puzzle" in the unknown because we lack mastery and competence as well as scripts of success, in the process of meeting the Other. The Other's otherness is our own challenge, due to lack of knowledge, humility, questioning, ideas of identity, superiority and our own lack of competence.

My point of departure

Diversity – good or bad?

Is diversity good or bad? This question has been tumbling around in managers' minds; it has stimulated research in many directions and fuelled energy in many ideological discussions. Logic tell us that diversity costs, and yet has potential. The question is whether the costs are less than the value of realised potential? And, if you are a manager, what can you do in order to reduce cost and increase the realised value. Meta-studies report more negative than positive experiences (Stahl et al., 2010; Stahl et al., 2015). However, we do not need to do what most people do. We can learn from the best. In seeking out best practice, reading about how many have unsuccessfully managed diversity vs successfully managed differences in teams and organisations is not that interesting or useful. The question is whether we can identify what practices lead to better results – and how people and organisations can learn and improve these best practices within their own context, and so improve their path to a better future.

My professional background

In this book I will draw on my 30 years of experience as a psychologist and organisational/managerial consultant. I have had a special dedication to "How to make teams work when participants are very different". The differences that have been my major focus are differences rooted in personality, in professional and educational scientific paradigms, and differences due to cultural background. Interpersonal, inter-disciplinary and cross-cultural are words that describe these three areas. My 30 years of practice have included lecturing at universities, cross-cultural research projects, and developing assessment products, and perhaps most importantly, more than 1,000 consultant engagements in 20 countries.

Diversity Icebreaker

During my last 25 years of experience, there is one concept that we have developed that has given me extraordinary experiences and positioning. This is a concept called Diversity Icebreaker. This concept combines the use of a psychologically based written questionnaire followed by a carefully designed experiential seminar. The questionnaire test maps how people have preferences in relation to how they apply information and interact with each other when solving problems in groups. As a result, the group is categorised according to stronger preferences in Red, Blue and Green. Through a highly interactive seminar lasting 60 plus minutes, the participants become deeply involved in creating their own local meaning of the colour categories. They create a rich/thick description and make the world colourful with Red, Blue and Green – not black, white, brown or yellow. These categories and the seminar are not only functional categories, they also have some implicit and explicit norms with respect to diversity, equality and complementarity. Thousands of consultants, leaders and change makers have used this concept when working with diversity, whether the diversity is due to personality, professional scientific paradigms, cultural background or any other diversity categories. The most typical contexts it is used in are personal development, communication, teams and projects, leadership and change management. Nevertheless, it has also been applied to promote a culture of innovation, of trust, such as in peace oriented initiatives in the Middle East, and cross-cultural and interdisciplinary research projects.

Since 1995, the Diversity Icebreaker has been promoted and developed by Human Factors AS, a Norwegian consultation company. When I write "we", the noun represents the group of employees in this organisation, the group that has collectively shared experiences, reflected together, and improved both the product and the research around the concept. There are two research volumes that have been published representing the academic contributions from this group and its network (Ekelund & Langvik, 2008; Ekelund & Pluta, 2015). When I write "I", it represents my own initiatives and positions I have taken in relation to my practice, my colleagues and customers.

Work life challenges

The majority of my experience with Diversity Icebreaker has been in professional organisational settings. The business case of diversity has been the overarching purpose, working to create better results. The rational model has been to utilise differences among people in the organisation in order to create a more valuable collective output. In these contexts, we have gradually seen that the concept also has relevance for individual self-development, acknowledgement, trust and positivity – areas of importance for living a good life. The use of Diversity Icebreaker in work life contexts has given me the possibility to facilitate discussions with participants in seminars eliciting ideals on how we shall communicate, work and live together in a way that promotes ethical behaviour and dignified development of individuals and groups.

To ask questions and elaborate alternative answers is a way of training collective reflection, which is an important practice that is needed in the development of ethical practice, public discourses and in creating a climate where individuals feel free to speak about alternative perspectives. Examples of questions at work that have general ethical parallels are: "What are our goals, really? What kind of norms do we need to mutually agree on to work together? Which metaphors and models inspire us? What type of communication supports people's self-development? What are our values and norms that make us an excellent organisation?"

These questions relate to life at work and are relevant in order to improve results. But, they are also relevant questions for people living in a community and society. These questions will be more challenging when the groups of people involved have quite different backgrounds. It will be more challenging when there are many Others. At the same time, the work place is probably one of the few places where adults systematically and frequently can ask these questions, develop their practice in asking such questions, and at the same time build collective competence to solve challenging situations together. For this reason, how we do this communication and solve problems together at work has a huge potential for spill over effects to other sectors. Private life is just one of the other areas where improved quality of communication from life at work can contribute to positive effects. For me, the possibility of contributing to a society with dignity in communicative practice has been one of my major motivations for promoting the use of Diversity Icebreaker. In this work, I have also had the possibility of seeing how a good communicative practice can lead to a higher quality of problem solving when addressing issues related to environmental concern as well as migration problems. If an increased application of Diversity Icebreaker were to lead to a more dignified problem solving in these areas, then I have achieved one important goal for the writing of this book.

In the beginning of the 1990s, I took part in the process of rebuilding the credibility of major financial institutions that had gone bankrupt. I facilitated dialogues, discussions and debates with a large degree of involvement in order to identify core values for leaders and employees. When the core values were identified as representing the important values and motivators for direction in the firm, the question was how to bring them alive. Employee surveys, feedback and reflexive discussions in groups were institutionalised as improvement strategies. Such kinds of processes have been growing in numbers in organisations.[2] Nowadays, I very often meet managers who are seriously talking and acting within value based inspirational platforms. And, as long as the organisation delivers satisfactory profit, I find these leaders more interested in doing good for employees, society and nature, than increasing profit even more. In my view, large degrees of involvement in life at work, combined with values based management is something that can contribute to build large numbers of citizens trained for decent dialogues, discussions and debates around such issues.

Another area of work life that is growing is international meetings, conferences and co-operative platforms across nations. This is especially relevant concerning climate issues, since water, air and heat do not show respect for country borders. In such settings, the capability of communicating effectively across all kinds of differences is paramount. In these settings, if the ambition is to create new solutions together, the importance of communicating in a way that integrates the "Others'" ideas is fundamental. The need for developing a way of working together that make these meetings and processes as effective and innovative as possible is of extreme importance for high quality end products. At the same time, these arenas are places where good communicative practices can be reinforced and strengthened. There are lots of positive spill over effects from successful international professional practice. Positive experiences increase belief in efficacy; this creates personal bonds across nations, leads to increased acceptance of "Others", and increases the communicative repertoire.

Case: Dubrovnik

In 2012 I kicked off a hugely complex EU research project: 58 participants, 28 organisations and 12 countries. The goal for the project was to identify future effects of increased sulphur dioxide in rain on objects with important cultural heritage in Europe. Besides the organisational and cultural diversity, there was a mixture of advanced researchers and data-harvesting fieldworkers. How could they start with some elements of common ground? I decided to apply the Diversity Icebreaker which in its classical form created both a shared language of diversity relevant for their problem solving. For me, seeing the effect for all involved, both at individual and collective level, reinforced my curiosity to understand the potential of such a process.

The nation as a political and economic unity is still an organisational form that is used as a key disaggregating factor in global agreements. Political representatives have to document their success back to those people that have elected them. Global business organisations cross borders and *may* act as institutions with financial goals every month as a constant target. Alternatively global organisations can also act with a long term global perspective, differentiated from many shorter term cyclical political systems. In my view I see an increasingly decent attitude evolving across many leaders where a willingness to take social and environmental issues into their spheres of concern is more prevalent. This strengthens my belief in the work life context as a very relevant and important place for developing dignified communication.

Dignity

In German the word "Bildung" is used to represent the formative part of the education where individuals develop their potential through taking part in social and cultural activities. Through reflective practice and being actively involved, they contribute to the collective growth of cultural institutions and practices. An ultimate goal for this book is to inspire people to be more competent to solve Grand[3] problems in collaboration with Others, and simultaneously increase the level of dignity in the communication and interaction. Questions like "Who am I? Who are you? How do we interact? What is our goal? How shall we distribute our resources?" are important questions that traditionally have been played out in families, religions, educational institutions and political institutions. The humanistic disciplines at universities have been one of the important areas for discussing these fundamental questions inside academic disciplines. Today, I think these are questions we all need to be involved in and responding to.[4] And, as mentioned above, I think the work-life context is the arena that now has a possibility to involve large numbers of adult people reflecting and discussing. In this book I will use examples from my work that I think contribute to more dignified practice and promotion of "Bildung".

Norway/Scandinavia as context

In Scandinavia, we have a social democratic culture with lots of top scores on welfare indicators. This cultural context is important to be aware of in understanding the development and growth of Diversity Icebreaker. More than half of the volume of Diversity Icebreaker seminars are in Norway, and the number grows every year. Even though my international work experience has been more extensive than many in Norway, I have been raised within a cultural background of non-affluent farmers and workers and Norway as a whole in my backbone. What aspects of Norway's cultural context is relevant in relation to Diversity Icebreaker?

First of all, I think a high degree of trust creates a feeling of safety, predictability, and the expectancy of being treated well. If you do wrong, people will hope for better luck next time. Context is very often used as an explanation for bad behaviour. We believe people can be trusted upfront. Trust is taken for granted. You have to disappoint many times to earn distrust.

Second, we have little intrinsic respect for hierarchy or given authority. People are free and expected to speak out if they are frustrated with the leader or the organisation. However, if you are in power, you need to be careful and kind. You do not have the same freedom. Power is not understood as something to show off. Be humble; if you are smart or rich, do not make a point out of it. The idea of "all being equal" is essential.

Third, we have a long tradition in large scale involvement of workers in change and developmental processes. This implies that it is easy to invite participants in the organisations to take charge. The involvement of workers as a democratic practice has influenced the ideas of promoting a meaningful and growth oriented workplace for the individuals. This industrial democracy with a focus on worker development influenced all Scandinavian countries from the early 1970s.

I state these elements in order to make you as a reader aware of the context from within which my emerging practice and development of Diversity Icebreaker emerged. Geert Hofstede has been repeatedly stating that without clarifying the cultural context, you reduce the possibility of being aware of limitations as well as the possibilities of disseminating practices across countries. The Diversity Icebreaker is the only original concept developed in Norway in the area of Human Resource Management that has spread globally. By 2017, 250,000 people in 70 countries have used the questionnaire and seminar processes.

Since 1994, I happen to have been able to remain central in developing, learning about and working with many others on the different applications and nuances of this concept, both in research and practice. I have become aware that this continuous thread makes it possible for me to share the evolution in a particularly unique way and take you on the journey as best as I can.

Notes

1 Anthropocene is the idea that states that when the history of the planet will be described due to geological analysis in the future, the time of human beings will be seen as a distinct time period, like Holocene and Pleistocene.....

2 Jørn Bue Olsen reported in his PhD that following the financial crisis in 2002/3 many large companies started to report "values" in their annual reports. This seems to be an increasing practice of concern for managers both for internal as well as external legitimacy (Olsen, 2006).

3 Grand challenges are more than ordinary research questions or priorities, they are end results or outcomes that are global in scale, challenging for people and planet.

4 In my city, Larvik in Norway, Thor Heyerdahl was born. He is most known for his excursions with Kon-Tiki and Ra I and Ra II where he wanted to demonstrate the possibility of ancient travels across continents. He was also known as a person who pointed out the destruction of oceans with oil and garbage. He appealed to the UN to address this pollution as a global challenge and wanted all nations to be involved in saving the seas. His call for a globalised cooperation to save the planet has inspired me and many others. In my city a group of tourist experts were asked to describe how

Thor Heyerdahl's name could be applied in a science centre. The group suggested in 2018 to create a humanistic science centre where Diversity Icebreaker was integrated as an exercise. The humanistic ambition to create self-awareness and reflexivity about self and others was seen as an important entrance to globalised engagement for both human beings and the environmental concern of the planet (Gjetrang, Jervan & Barber, 2018).

Bibliography

Casey, M.E. & Robinson, S.M. (2017). *Neuroscience of Inclusion. New Skills for New Times*. Denver: Outskirts Press

Ekelund, B.Z. & Langvik, E. (Eds.) (2008). *Diversity Icebreaker: How to Manage Diversity Processes*. Oslo: Human Factors Publishing

Ekelund, B.Z. & Pluta, P. (Eds.) (2015). *Diversity Icebreaker II. Further Perspectives*. Oslo: Human Factors Publishing

Fukuyama, F. (2014). *Political Order and Political Decay: From the Industrial Revolution to the Present Day*. New York: Farrar, Straus and Giroux

Furnham, A., Steele, H. & Pendleton, D. (1993) A psychometric assessment of the Belbin Team-Role Self Perception Inventory. *Journal of Occupational and Organizational Psychology*, 66: 245–257

Gjetrang, K., Jervan, B. & Barber, S. (2018). *THINK - Thor Heyerdahl International Knowledge Centre. A report (feasibility study) on a Thor Heyerdahl humanistic science centre*. Delivered to Larvik Municipality January 2018

Hariri, Y.N. (2014). *Sapiens. A Brief History of Humankind*. New York: Harper

Hariri, Y.N. (2015). *Homo Deus. A Brief History of Tomorrow*. London, UK: Harwill Secker

Lifegate (2018). Syria, the environmental crisis behind the civil war. https://www.lifegate.com/people/news/syria-the-environmental-crisis-behind-the-civil-war. Last viewed 30 Nov. 2018

Olsen, J.B. (2006). *Om doble normer i næringslivet – etikken I tidsklemma*. PhD, School of Commerce at Gøteborg University.

Said, E.W. (1979). *Orientalism*. New York: Vintage Books

Stahl, G.K., Miska, C., Hyun-Jung, L., de Luque, M.S. (2015). The upside of cultural differences: Towards a more balanced treatment of culture in cross-cultural management research. Call for Papers for a Special Issue in *Cross Cultural & Strategic Management*

Stahl, G.K., Maznevski, M.L., Voigt, A. & Jonsen, K. (2010). Unravelling the effects of cultural diversity in teams: A meta-analysis of research on multicultural work groups. *Journal of International Business Studies*, 41(4): 690–709

Steinbeck, J. (1952). *East of Eden*. London: Penguin Books

UNCHR (2016). Global trends: Forced displacement in 2016. http://www.unhcr.org/globaltrends2016/. Last visited 30 Nov. 2018

UNHCR (2018). Europe situation. http://www.unhcr.org/europe-emergency.html?gclid=CjwKCAjw85zdBRB6EiwAov3Rijlwk5_F89_cA9zxXffRJb-v8oqD6Ia2X7Nw4Gd24EnqLOmce9lhuhoCQQAQAvD_BwE&gclsrc=aw.ds. Last visited 13 April 2018

2 Red, Blue and Green and Diversity Icebreaker

The evolution from underlying principles

Introduction

In this chapter, I will introduce Red, Blue and Green as categories of diversity that describe differences between the way people treat information when solving problems together. The categories are presented as categories of deep level diversity that are socially constructed in contrast to surfaced level categories of diversity. The starting point of Red, Blue and Green was three different communication strategies applied for reducing energy consumption. I trace the history from 1995 to developing the design of the classical Diversity Icebreaker seminar in 2003. The different communicative qualities and values of Red, Blue and Green are described. Examples are given from learning processes and insights from the meetings between people with different colours. Advice is shared for communicating well across colours. The internal dynamics between the three colours are described with ideas for how to promote integrated personal development.

Diversity categories in organisations

> Many Europeans don't share the same understanding of what Americans mean by diversity. In many European languages, the closest word to it emphasizes differences and implies categorization, partition, and separation …
>
> (Bloom, 2002:48)

Diversity management is a concept that often is used in organisations where the focus is on how to avoid discrimination against individuals from minority groups, or from a group that does not have the same equal opportunity to compete in the job market. The aim is to be more inclusive of the Others. The UK governmental policies have focused on ethnic minorities, gender, age, sexual orientation, religion and physical and mental disabilities in their benchmarks. But, even these categories are not the same type of category. They have very different starting points and qualities. Some of them have genetic foundations. The starting point is biological, but, then it turns into an interplay of biological and social stereotyping and experience through family, community, organisational and cultural interactions as you grow up and engage fully with society.

The socialised conceptualisation of race and gender, what they imply and how they play out differs in different countries. For example, being a woman has different career consequences in southern Europe than in northern Europe. Sexual orientation has genetic physiological roots and then is partly culturally defined and ultimately an individual choice. Religious differences are personal, social and collective constructs with deep implications for personal identity, groups, nations and sadly, long lasting conflicts.

More recently categories of diversity have been conceptualised in a much broader way. In the *Global Diversity & Inclusion Benchmarks* [1]

> *Diversity* refers to the variety of similarities and differences among people, including, but not limited to: gender, gender identity, ethnicity, race, native or indigenous origin, age, generation, sexual orientation, culture, religion, belief system, marital status, parental status, socio-economic difference, appearance, language and accent, disability, mental health, education, geography, nationality, work style, work experience, job role and function, thinking style, and personality type.
>
> (O'Hare & Richter, 2017: 1)

Defining diversity in this way includes almost all types of individual and group differences. And, such a broader definition includes the diversity categories of Red, Blue and Green in Diversity Icebreaker.

In order to have a fair society where the many different aspects that make up any one individual (now termed "intersectionality") are treated with respect and afforded equal opportunities for a good life, different measures need to be taken in order to re-balance social inequalities. Affirmative action and positive discrimination are policies meant to compensate for historical inequalities in certain specific aspects of diversity. They are laudable, yet difficult and do not always end with a satisfactory outcome for minority and marginalised groups (Sabharwal, 2014).

From surface-level diversity to deep-level categories of diversity

In this book I will not focus upon the policies of management or societal bodies set up to avoid negative effects for the groups mentioned in the more narrow categorisation of diversity. My use of the concept of diversity is not rooted in biological or social distinctions, but in a holistic individual, yet common, cognitive framework that has a different internalised foundation for categorisation. What does it mean? Here are some examples of comments from participants illustrating how a Diversity Icebreaker intervention lessens the focus on biological and social diversity categories, while providing a safe platform from which to explore their possible impact.

From UK I received an anonymous message from a participant who had taken part in a seminar related to sexual preferences. *"This Diversity Icebreaker exercise made it not that easy to see who was gay."*

Annika Khano stated after a Diversity Icebreaker seminar with Israelis, Jordanians and Palestinians. *"Diversity Icebreaker helped the teachers to overcome personal restraints and suspicions. The Diversity Icebreaker created a different sense of belonging among the participants, dividing them into colours rather than into nationalities. Thus, the issue of being Israeli, Palestinian or Jordanian took a back seat and left enough room for the teachers to integrate into new groups, independently of their national identity. .... the creation of a 'third culture' highly contributed to the positive atmosphere of the workshop and the big 'elephant' inside the room – the Israeli-Arab conflict – became almost invisible."*

Does this imply that I think we seek to ignore these differences? No, absolutely not. It is important to address any salient categories to analyse and re-align in the face of injustice. Affirmative Action strategies are a compensatory consequence of analysing these roots of historical injustice. For instance, in Norway, 40% of board members in a public listed company must be women. But, there are times when highlighting certain differences does not add value. There are situations where focusing on minority or marginalised group qualities leads to reinforced attention and potential tensions of who are perceived as insiders and who as outsiders. The categories and initiatives seems to have a reinforcing effect of stigmatising the minority groups just due to the implicit values in the language, as well as the initiatives. When minority groups are recruited due to a quota, it can have consequences for that person's social image and sense of personal self-worth in the assigned roles.[2]

In order to understand the quality of the Red, Blue and Green categories in Diversity Icebreaker, I have to introduce the difference between categories of diversity that can emerge into visible physiological as well as psychological and emotional differences, and those that remain internal, but that we guess at by observing someone's behaviour. I will call these surfaced versus internal diversities. A surfaced level diversity is something that is visibly different, like different levels and types of melanin in the skin and other physical features that imply different ethno-geographical ancestries and origins; physiologically visible gender differences and guessing someone's age from their physical features.

Then there are some diversity categories that are not physically seen, but are internal cognitive phenomena that influence someone's perception, language, choices and behaviour. Such internalised diversity categories are things like cultural values, personality, scientific paradigms, organisational values etc. The categories of Red, Blue and Green may have some biological determinants (refer to personality, cognitive style) – however they are not perceptible at the physiologically surfaced level, but rather expressed through a person's behaviour and choices.

Diversity Icebreaker categories are also perceived to have different meanings in different cultures. In some societies being the person who suggests changes, a typical quality of someone with a Green preference, is perceived as creative. In other societies it can be seen as a critique of the establishment. Red, Blue and Green have such deep internal elements.

In the classical Diversity Icebreaker seminar, the test/questionnaire assesses qualities that are rooted in individual values, traits and capabilities. Following the assessment, participants are grouped with others with the same dominant qualities, and then, at that time – in that space, they socially define the meaning of their specific category often critiquing and exploring of the questions in the questionnaire. They formulate ideas from within and from outside after being grouped according to their dominant colour. For example those with a dominant Red preference describe themselves first and then Blue and Green. From the beginning, the categories of Red, Blue and Green are introduced as categories that are relevant for interaction. Even though Red, Blue and Green are rooted in deep level diversity phenomena, the categories become meaningful and definable in a communicative exchange of ideas. The categories can best be described as "socially constructed deep level categories".

There is another quality that is essential with Red, Blue and Green and contrasts with the classical surfaced categories of gender, race, etc. In many of these categories, you either belong or do not. Despite much progress to understand a more continuous reality, many people still expect you to be a either man or woman. You are either heterosexual or LGBTQ, a Christian or a non-Christian. You are raised in one country and not the other. Despite so many examples of in-betweens, categorisation is a process that intrinsically excludes the "Others" and for this reason needs a constructed compensatory process of inclusion. Ironically, those who need and most often want inclusion, are the ones that are victimised by the people and/or the processes that exclude.

In contrast, Diversity Icebreaker diversifies people by showing each person which colour is their main preference. Each individual has all three colours as personal qualities at different levels of preference. This makes it possible to see the Other's primary preference through the lenses of one's own non-dominant preferences. Red, Blue and Green are categories that diversify and unify at the same time. They are categories of diversity from deep within each of us, yet everyone has the three colours in common. In social interaction, at best, people with different primary preferences need each other to solve problems. While differentiating, the Diversity Icebreaker process simultaneously unifies across all individuals by sharing the fact that we need people with the three different colour preferences to solve a complex problem. Their complimentary qualities invite a sense of underlying unity stretching through the social interaction. At the collective level, each person in the whole group is unified, while diversified at individual level and yet still belonging to the whole group. They are a part of the Gestalt.

This is possible, because unlike other categorisation processes, the Diversity Icebreaker categories of Red, Blue and Green do not exclude. For this reason, "re-inclusion" is not an issue when these categories are applied. This fundamentally inclusive quality makes the categories of Diversity Icebreaker systematically different from categories founded on visible and less visible physiological and socially constructed differences, like "race, ethnic/cultural background, gender, sexual orientation, religion, and genetic, physical and mental differences".

The inclusive categories of Diversity Icebreaker bring the potential for building an all-inclusive community, where people see what they have in common. Ironically the language of Red, Blue and Green creates trust and hope for future problem solving where everyone is involved. "Reframing Others in Colours of Mastery" is one of our conference titles that is inspired by these qualities (Ekelund & Pluta, 2017). This unique quality of simultaneously differentiating and unifying enables Red, Blue and Green to be useful for business purposes as well as addressing and solving the problems underlying the Grand challenges.

As mentioned, traditional diversity management practice has sometimes been triggered by human rights and anti-discriminatory initiatives. However, often the business case fuels the arguments because of the overlap between the ideas of human rights and business goals in some situations. If more diverse people are involved, we have the potential for more diverse perspectives and access to a much broader set of competences. This is what we call "the resource perspective" in economic theory.

Managing increased resources well can lead to better results. If we exclude one type of worker, for example women, then we have fewer resources to draw on. Japan struggles these days because the country competes in the global market with a relatively low number of women involved in work life. The value of women employed in Norway, proportionately higher than in most OECD countries, is estimated to be higher than the value of Norwegian oil/gas/pension fund (Stoltenberg, 2013; Dept of Finance, 2013).

The Diversity Icebreaker categories of Red, Blue and Green are cognitive styles that all people have but use in different degrees. This is a holistic individual perspective. If we look at Red, Blue and Green as ways of categorising people into different groups based upon their primary preference for "treating information in problem solving groups", then we have a concept that diversifies people. If we understand the problem-solving process as a process where all categories are needed, then the categories unify within that process across people. If we see the whole process as a metaphor, we can ask what are the main qualities in this metaphor and how does this mirror the realities of life, leading to discussions about equality and complementarity as one example. Added to that, it seems that the Diversity Icebreaker seminar per se – not the categories, but the seminar – creates positivity, increased creativity and trust (Arieli et al., 2018).

Here is an illustration of how the main elements in this book are connected.

In this illustration I have presented on the left side the traditional categories of diversity management from a social justice perspective. Sometimes they are surfaced diversities, too, but not always. The internal deep level diversities in the next column are areas that I will discuss systematically in this book. I will also show how the different Red, Blue and Green categories can promote efficiency, innovation as well as an inclusive community. I have listed the three different goals of efficiency, innovation and inclusive community as they resonate with the qualities of Red, Blue and Green as elicited in the Diversity

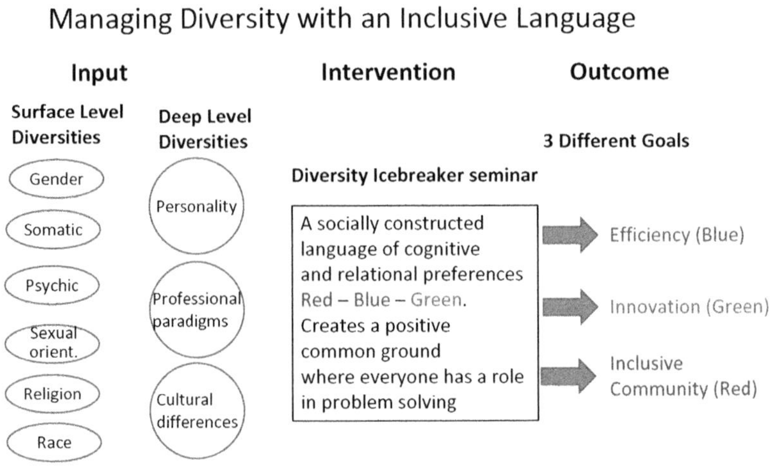

Managing Diversity with an Inclusive Language

Input		Intervention	Outcome

Surface Level Diversities | **Deep Level Diversities** | | **3 Different Goals**

Gender

Personality

Somatic

Psychic

Professional paradigms

Sexual orient.

Religion

Cultural differences

Race

Diversity Icebreaker seminar

A socially constructed language of cognitive and relational preferences
Red – Blue – Green.
Creates a positive common ground where everyone has a role in problem solving

Efficiency (Blue)

Innovation (Green)

Inclusive Community (Red)

Figure 2.1 Managing diversity with an inclusive language

Icebreaker seminar. The chapters in this book are directly linked to these internal diversity areas and how Red, Blue and Green play out in relation to the three different type of goals.

The evolution of Diversity Icebreaker and Red, Blue and Green

Diversity Icebreaker and Red, Blue and Green emerged as categories through a consultative challenge given to a group of four consulting companies in 1994. I was invited to take part due to my background in psychology. Our client provided electricity to all households in the community. One of the departments in the organisation had 70 engineers who were responsible for giving advice to consumers to enable them to use less energy. The manager of this department phrased the challenge: "We have already talked with those customers who were interested in energy conservation and they have done what they can do. Now we need to reach out with our message to other segments in our customer portfolio with a communication that leads to real change." I was recommended to create focus groups with the client's customer in order to better understand the end user position.

I decided to include a process in the focus groups named "Brainwriting Pool". This was a process where silent idea-generation was combined with building upon each other's ideas, a process Van Gundy (1981) recommended which prevented the negative effects of social dynamics in normal brainstorming. The question I asked in the focus groups was "How can energy conservation advisors communicate in a way that leads to behavioural change among customers?"

In order to sort the ideas, I used the principles from qualitative methodology, grounded theory described by Strauss & Corbin (1990), where ideas are sorted based upon whether the ideas are alike or different. But, instead of having me as a researcher doing this categorisation, I asked the customers themselves to make this analysis. I arranged three different focus groups. Each of the focus groups organised three main categories of similar character that covered about 90% of the ideas. A decision was made to use these categories as three main strategies in marketing and consultation. We had some ideas that they represented different segments in the market. We dared not differentiate communication in a way that exclusively targeted defined market segments with specific communication. Instead we trained 70 advisors with engineering backgrounds to identify patterns in the communication with a single customer and then apply the differentiated strategies in each individual case. The categories were named Red, Blue and Green. This was partly due to similarities in the motivation for energy conservation in different political parties in Norway, and partly due to inspiration of colour use seen in the Team Management Profile concept developed by Dick McCann and Charles Margerison (Margerison & McCann, 1991; McCann, 1988).

Green arguments were based upon environmental concern and willingness to take on large changes. Blue arguments were based upon economy and control. Red arguments were rooted in social acceptance and role modelling. A campaign actively reached out to 15,000 households with interactive communication. The energy consumption in the county was reduced in next five months at a value of four million dollars, five times as much as the cost of the whole campaign. It was one of the first effective documented energy conservation campaigns in Norway (Ekelund, 1997).[3]

Due to the success of this campaign we were asked to make a customer analysis. In order to identify which category was dominant in different customer segments, we created a simple questionnaire (Hegge, 1997). Questions were picked from different assessments related to learning and communication styles, team roles and personality. Some 100 people answered 100 questions and statistically clustered those 15 questions that co-varied inside each of the categories and differentiated in between them. We delivered multiple analyses for the customer using this assessment.

In my company one of our main areas of work at that time was assessment and training of teams. The questionnaire we made to identify whether the customers had Red, Blue or Green preferences looked like a very simple team role model. For this reason, we integrated this in our team training (Ekelund and Jørstad, 1998). The team role concept in more advanced and scientific forms was formulated by Belbin (1981) and Margerison & McCann (1991).

Our assessment of Red, Blue and Green did not yet have the scientific backing of these concepts. For this reason, we only talked about the mapping of Red, Blue and Green as a way of introducing the main models of thinking around the ideas of team roles: "People are different. These differences have implications for motivation and success in different roles in teamwork." Even so, our model of Red, Blue and Green was different from established team roles concept – and because we did not have at that time a high quality of statistical rigour in the description of the test – we started to involve participants in a different exercise to put more meat on the bones.

We elaborated and expanded the understanding of Red, Blue and Green in different situations. We repeatedly focused on how perceptions of Red, Blue and Green varied from inside and outside, or from an actor vs observer perspective the way it is phrased by Jones & Nisbett (1972). We created groups based on the dominant score in one of the colours as the criteria for belonging. The processes of describing oneself and the Other, with positive and/or negative tendencies, had an enormously speedy group dynamic effect. Labelling combined with the development of group cohesion processes evolved almost every time. However, in contrast with what we had seen described in social science literature, these groups developed identity concepts with humour, self-irony and reflection. When we saw this happen, we realised the value of the seminar construction as a pedagogical tool. The combination of an assessment as the starting point of an immersive participatory seminar seemed to create learning points in a relatively complex area: Learning of importance to both practice as well as theoretical understanding. The seminar gradually grew in consistency, and we started to name it Diversity Icebreaker seminar. Later on when variety grew, we named the seminar the classical Diversity Icebreaker seminar. The definition of the classical core is the four step process of testing, group work in mono-coloured groups, sharing in between groups, and collective reflection.

Our experience in different settings, plus feedback from other consultants who replicated our work, indicated that this could be a future success. In 1999 we applied the concept outside Norway for the first time in Bosnia-Herzegovina. It was then used to create a common experience and shared language among representatives from the three local culturally diverse groups with additional international representatives (Maznevski & Ekelund, 2004). Well aware of the deep challenges in cross-cultural interaction, we also saw the potential for global application. In 2003 we decided to do more rigorous research around the assessment and the seminar. In 2005 we decided to "go global" and started to involve researchers and consultants outside Norway to develop knowledge and practice relevant for the global market (Ekelund & Langvik, 2008). Now, in 2018, it has been used by more than 250,000 people in 70 different countries.

Case: Entrepreneur history

Many times entrepreneurship success stories are illustrated as a very goal directed activity. Other times accidental events are highlighted as important factors. In the development of Diversity Icebreaker to a global success there are many elements that were unpredictable and not foreseen as the story evolved. We did not see what could happen around the next corner. We did not see how new experiences created new ideas for other perspectives, enlarged our knowledge and created areas for future application. What has evolved was a consequence of an innovative business strategy. Stepwise innovation has been fuelled by a combination of reflecting and learning from our own diversified experiences and groups of participants repeatedly asking questions. Questions such as: "What is happening here? How can we see this in another way? How can we test these new ideas both in practice and in more scientific ways? How can we share these ideas in our global network to test the generalisability?" If we were to describe the main innovative steps retrospectively, they are:

1   Red, Blue and Green were established as three distinct categories in 1995 for marketing and behavioural change purposes. They were used to train engineers to use more diversified communication strategies in order to facilitate behavioural change among energy consumption consumers.
2   The request to make customer analyses necessitated creating an assessment tool to categorise the customers in either Red, Blue or Green preferences.
3   The assessment looked like a team role concept and was integrated into the training programs of team consultants.
4   Since the assessment was that simple, we decided to add exercises to make broader and richer descriptions.
5   When we saw the effects of labelling and emerging group dynamics we realised the potential for experiential learning around categorisation, stereotyping, group dynamics, actor–observer differences and meeting with the Others.
6   When we saw the positive reactions in the market, we understood the global potential.

Description of Red, Blue and Green

Red, Blue and Green is about individual differences. What type of differences? This is a question we often get. In seminars we simply suggest that you will learn about yourself. Many participants assume that this is a personality test. But, personality is a very broad concept and when psychologists create a test of personality they would like to describe all the facets that they think systematically differ between people. Big 5 (Costa & McCrae, 1992) is today one of the models that is most often recommended within the personality assessment area.

We look upon personality as a more base level phenomena; as a broad platform playing a formative role in individuals' life and behaviour. We think that personality influences Red, Blue and Green. Indeed studies have been done where the Red, Blue and Green categories have been correlated with Big 5 dimensions. We have also studied how Red, Blue and Green interconnect with values, cognitive style, cultural values and emotional intelligence (Ekelund & Langvik, 2008). We keep on pursuing this psychological research tradition. But, given what we know of the history of the concept – and later research – we say that Red, Blue and Green is about "how we treat information differently when we are solving problems together in groups". This is more in line with how Red, Blue and Green emerged out of ideas for how you can communicate in order to change the Other's behaviour (engineers talking with customers in order to make them use less energy). Those who are Blue have a preference for details, figures and plans. Red for relations, feelings and community. Green is about the big picture, new ideas and changes.

In psychological terms we say that Red, Blue and Green is about preferences. The research tell us that personality, values and cognitive style influences these preferences (Ekelund & Pluta, 2015). In practice it implies that Red, Blue and Green have implications for how you see and approach tasks and people – and that your most likely default reaction is usually aligned with your preferences.

When you meet Others your perception of them will be formed by your way of seeing the world. As mentioned in the former chapter, to see the Others from their own perspective is something you can do only if you have some knowledge about the Others and their context. Most people get access to this knowledge through communication. Of course, the more experience you get with different Others, the more alternative and complex views are accessible for you. But, your own colour preference becomes the starting point. It is very difficult to imagine that being otherwise. So, the next step is to approach the Other in order to learn more about their perspective, perceived context, background, values etc. It is about having the ability to see the Other's position with empathy. 'Mentalisation' is the concept that has emerged in psychology in recent years, to describe the process of making sense of another person's subjective status and processes. It is the capability to see things from the Other's perspective, which is the starting point of integrating the other person's view and perspectives including learning about oneself through the eyes of Others.

In the next chapters I will explain why we react towards others based upon a usually less conscious awareness of alike or not, friend or enemy, positive or negative. Gradually we increase the ability to see the Others in more elaborated ways. Behavioural experiences lead to changes in our knowledge and emotions. Behaviour, cognition and emotions seem to influence each other in a complex interactive way. Research has identified different processes that can lead to openness and change. Psychological safety is an example of a concept that resonated for us when we saw people's willingness to reflect, learn and voice new ideas (Edmondson, 1999; Anderson & West, 1994). Seeing oneself from the point of the Other is a reframing process that is one of the important dialectical processes in personal development (Løvlie-Schibbye, 1983, 1985).

Red, Blue and Green are cognitive categories, language constructs, that are being constructed by the participants in each seminar. People create a shared understanding by applying the categories retrospectively, in the communication then and there and in planning processes for the future. In organisations that have applied Red, Blue and Green consistently over time, we have seen that the categories become a part of their language, relevant for categorising not only people but also tasks, processes and perspectives (Ekelund et al., 2015). The categories become a language system, a metaphorical structure, that has implications for seeing, communicating, acting and reflecting. Let me share with you one of the comments that I received some months after a man had taken part in a Diversity Icebreaker seminar. He said: *"My wife stopped being a problem when I understood she was Green."* In this sentence there are elements of different learning points. First of all he states that it is his own perspective that is central, not her qualities. And, when his perspective changed, his wife moved from a category of being problematic to *not* being problematic. The change in perception made him see future interaction in a more positive perspective with fewer problems and more easy-going interaction. He felt a positive mastery through imagining this more positive future interaction. The title "Reframe the Other in colours of mastery" for one of our conference presentations was inspired by this statement (Ekelund & Pluta, 2017). He himself had a strong Blue preference, and seeing his wife through his Blue lenses made her look challenging. She was not predictable, often changing perspectives on issues he had thought they had settled days before. However, when he realised that this was due to her preference for seeing alternatives and new opportunities, and not a way of forgetting the history, then he could follow up on her activities and integrate earlier discussions and experiences into the dialogues. He was able to master their interaction with respect for her, yet without leaving history behind. We often get feedback where participants share the same experience of increased mastery due to reorganising their own perception with Red, Blue and Green. How to effectively engage with the Other's difference is something that can be mastered in your own mind.

In the first seminar booklet in 2008 we created descriptions of Red, Blue and Green categories based upon the early years of research (Ekelund & Rydningen, 2008): They were as follows.

People with Red preference

People with a strong red preference enjoy spending time with other people. They have a lot of friends, and get energy from being together with people and from dialogue. To reach them it is important to have a personal and enthusiastic message. They easily achieve a secure and open conversation with new people. They are open about their feelings and find it easy to talk about them with others. At the same time, they show respect and patience towards others. Harmony in social settings is the most important thing to them, which may lead to concrete tasks being given lower priority. The goal of communication is to ensure inclusion and solidarity. They tend to be spontaneous and impulsive when meeting other people. They are often described as warm and easy-going, with the ability to create security and positive feelings among people.

They consider the emotional part to be more important than action and concrete ideas. Not only do they consider it important, but being able to be near as well as clear about their own feelings is one of their strengths. In addition, they may be aware that they or others might take up too much space and attention in the group. This ability, however, makes them successful when having an integrating role in groups; they make certain there is integration and respect in spite of the members' differences. They appear socially responsible, at the same time as they are concerned with having respect for each individual person. They are less ambitious in reaching goals and they may be difficult to get to contribute in a focused manner over time. Historical facts and sharp analysis are less important to them compared to creating a solution through conversation here and now. They can often be self-sacrificing in their pursuit of satisfaction and harmony.

People with Blue preference

People with a strong Blue preference are concerned with being concrete and practical. They like to calculate and work towards solutions in a systematic manner. They want things to be useful and serve a purpose. The aim of communication is to solve tasks in a precise way. In decision-making processes they want the facts to be presented and they measure the arguments in terms of usefulness and goal achievement. They are concerned with keeping the end result precise and all details correct.

They tend to think and consider the consequences before they say or do something concrete. They are good at being focused and goal-oriented, with the purpose of completing a task. They are not socially dominant, and are not ones to talk about feelings much or to be swept away by the world of imagination. They do not seek excitement for its own sake and are not carried away by torrents of positive emotion. Their everyday life is not characterised by impulsiveness, and spontaneous suggestions are mostly seen as disturbances. What has been done in the past is considered important when deciding what to do in the future. It is more important to carry on according to plan than be flexible and open to new and creative ideas. Their practical and down-to-earth style limits their openness for different kinds of experiences. They are conscientious and reliable, and gain trust over time. Conscientiousness and self-discipline are combined with a certain degree of orderliness. Carefulness and reliability are virtues to them.

Blue people are considerate to what the group wants and contribute constructively and consciously to the common good, and can in these situations show a great degree of loyalty, both concerning the group, the leader and the organisation. They do not want conflict, but seek productive and harmonious cooperation with few diversions. People with a blue preference are often seen as organised, focused, rational and without unnecessary emotional outbursts or a need to stand out in social contexts.

People with Green preference

People with a strong green preference are easily triggered by new ideas and the possibility of being able to do things differently. Unusual and untraditional ideas and solutions set their enthusiasm on fire. They enjoy looking deeply into a question or issue at the same time as they look for the overall picture and new angles from which to tackle their task. This enables them to often come up with imaginative solutions that connect ideas from different areas. They are ambitious and have high goals, often with a far-reaching perspective of tomorrow's possibilities.

They tend to make their mark quickly, often with thoughts and ideas that can dominate and influence what to focus on later. They are very open to new ways of thinking and new ideas, and are easily carried away or lead abstract and exciting discussions. Being impulsive and creative is their every-day mode. They may use feelings and beauty as both inspiration and reason-ing for what they find important. They do not think for long or evaluate the consequences before they speak or act. They are good at focusing on alter-native solutions while brainstorming, but are not necessarily those who have the patience to complete a task. Self-discipline, patience, order, details, or being conscientious do not characterise their everyday life. They can be socially dominant and do not always adapt to the group's prevailing ideas. Independence is one of their many strong values and they express their values easily, even when they are in opposition to those who are leading the group. Modesty is not a virtue to them and it is unlikely for them to make sacrifices for the organisation or community unless connected to strong, value based activities.

The beauty of positive perspectives

In the descriptions above we have mostly highlighted the positive sides of the personal qualities, not the negative, challenging or dark side. If you receive this positive message it is more acceptable than the opposite. It also creates a communication focus where positive qualities are highlighted. You will expect the Others to see you, as you see them, with a positive view. This has a positive reinforcing spiral effect. It leads to a wish for being together and to exchange information, knowledge and perspectives. We have seen that this effect leads to organisational cultures that promote posi-tive motivation, creativity, innovation, team work and loyalty. We see such positive "YES" cultures as being more prevalent in sports teams, sales orga-nisations, and in creative businesses like marketing. There are some organi-sations that work with marginalised people, early school leavers, retraining for work, etc., that also have the same pedagogical platform in order to build a culture that promotes positive self-identity through positive acknowl-edgment and feedback.

If you expect to be met by the Others in a positive way, it increases your willingness to voice, expose yourself, and be involved. If you expect the opposite, you would rather refrain from showing up, speaking up, and offering your competence to the benefit of the group. The expectation of being treated well by the Others when you yourself are vulnerable is the core of trust. I will introduce more about trust-building interaction in Chapter 9.

The need for the Other's feedback

As mentioned above, we have focused on the positive sides of Red, Blue and Green preferences. This increases the acceptance, builds positive identity and creates a culture where positive expectations in the interaction rules.

Focusing too strongly on the positive side can of course lead to an unrealistic self-enhanced self-image. One can become blind to the negative sides, as well as the impact of one's own negative or shadow character towards Others. Even when people behave their best in their own perspective, it might lead to negative effects towards Others and in the interaction.

This is something that might be difficult to reconcile. I joke, but with serious meaning, that it is difficult for dominant Green people to understand that they add most value by just saying nothing. Sometimes people with a strong Green preference have to step behind in order to let Others lead the interaction. Sometimes the Green has to let the qualities of Red and Blue form the processes. This can be hard when one is proud of oneself as a highly esteemed idea contributor. It is important to be attentive and flexible to the situation and the process. More of this in Chapter 6.

Learning from Others

Learning from Others' negative views about yourself is a way of adjusting your self-image closer to the social reality, the way it is seen by Others. Such "constructive" feedback functions much better following a positive exchange and when the ideas are explored jointly with curiosity and trust. Trust means, "I say it, because it can help you." In this safely held environment, everyone can search for the balance between hubris and humbleness, between Hercules and Buddha (Lane et al., 2004).

In leadership developmental programs, the Johari window was a popular model to train sensitivity and learning from Others (Luft & Ingham, 1955). The Johari window is a 2x2 square form illustrating the differences between what you and I can see.[4] Through feedback from Others you can increase your insights about what Others see but you do not. These are often named "blind spots", and where Others really are the sources of enlightened self-understanding. Such feedback can be aligned with what you can receive from a therapist, comments that make you question and explore your own subconscious motives; *"It seems to me that you are easily triggered into an opposing position? Why is this so?"* Such questioning and feedback can also make you more aware of the effect of your behaviour on Others. *"The way you express yourself makes me feel ignored. I feel I would like to pull back and not continue with this communication. I do not want to spend more energy on this – if you continue the same way."*

The Other's perspective might *not* be absolutely right, nevertheless, there are often elements that with curiosity can be explored in order to search for learning points. Anyhow, it might relevant to accept that such perspectives are "right" seen from the Other's perspective. Learning about these issues will increase your precision in perceiving and manoeuvring in social interaction.

I have analysed results from 50 seminars and identified the major issues that can be provocatively stated in strong negative wording. I have organised them in relation to "which colour does this feedback come from. It looks like this.

- Red might be seen from a Green perspective: Over sensitive. Talks themself out of it. Easy to influence. Takes too much time and space. Not serious enough.
- Red might be seen from a Blue perspective: Annoying when it comes to talking. Emotionally demanding. Decisions are based on feelings. The processes are more important than the result. Avoids conflict. Follows the wind.
- Blue might be seen from a Green perspective: Detail oriented. Rule fixated and follows routines. Schedules and time limits. Lacks fantasy. Safe on the inside of the box. Afraid of risk. Takes on too much responsibility.
- Blue might be seen from a Red perspective: Keep their emotions for themselves. Cold. Don't care about people. Boring and geeky. Rigid and square headed. Holding Other people back. Too sure about their own knowledge.
- Green might be seen from a Blue perspective: Unreliable and whimsy. Superficial. Difficult to understand. Chaotic. Up in the clouds. Both legs planted in the air. Big words. Occasionally hopeless.
- Green might be seen from a Red perspective: Daydreamers. Poor listening skills. Works too much. Not good at getting people on-board. Lacks patience. Insensitive. Individualistic.

Case: How interaction between Red, Blue and Green might happen

The Blues have arrived at the meeting in time, having read the minutes from last meeting, the agenda and having prepared what to say. Red and Green people arrive a bit late, but expect to receive acknowledgement for attending. A Green person suggests a new topic that recently has come to her mind as very important. She is not happy when this is put at the end of the agenda. She voices that this topic of hers will create another understanding of the suggested topics. A Red person interrupts with a helpful idea of making a compromise and asks if the issue could be integrated in one of the already accepted topics on the agenda. Time goes on with half-way discussions about the topic and how it could eventually fit in. The Blues are frustrated by the time lost. Two hours was the allocated time, and suddenly half an hour was gone without starting at the first point at the agenda. The Blues want to stick to the agenda, and are as a consequence accused of being unnecessarily rigid. The Others try to reach out for flexibility by saying that a rigid agenda is not what creates economic value in the organisation, so why be upset?

Positive experiences with blind spots

In the above examples we have illustrated Others as a possible source for understanding personal qualities that can have negative side effects. Others can also make us aware of *positive* contributions that we are not aware of. Often this happens when the feedback given to the Others is based upon the value system of oneself, and not what is important for the Others. Here are some examples.

- Red says to Green: Your energy and enthusiasm make it more attractive to be a member of this team.
- Blue says to Red: Your interest for my plan make me motivated to improve the plan to a higher level of detail.
- Green says to Blue: Your way of systematising all the details make me see a total new solution.

Different contexts, different preferences lead to different evaluations of the same phenomena.

Flexibility in your roles

In some psychological tests there is a tradition to allocate individual qualities on one or the other side of a scale. An example is the extrovert versus introvert in the models built on Carl Gustav Jung. From what we know from test psychology of individual traits, this is not true. Most traits are distributed in the population as they are distributed in a Gauss curve of distribution (Furnham, 1993). Some people are extreme – but quite a lot score in the middle for example on the degree of extroversion. Grant introduced the label Advert on those people in the middle and showed empirically that they were more successful in sales than extroverts (Grant, 2013). Sometimes factors that look like polarities are positioned as opposites. In some cases this is not true either. An example of this might be the polarities of thinking versus feeling. These two categories are two different functions, but in practice they are not opposites when we talk about individual preferences or capacities.

Red, Blue and Green are individual traits, or preferences in a more precise wording. In our model we position them as separate qualities that differentiate them from each other, but not as a continuum on a scale. In teamwork, we focus on what is the highest preference for each person in their internal dynamics, and then we search for roles and activities in the team that are aligned with this preference. At the same time, we highlight that it is very rare for anyone to score almost zero on any of the colour preferences. Most people are able to utilise their qualities belonging to the second and third preference when it is needed. We have made some badges that underline this triple quality of each person.

On the Red badge is written in small letters "...but also Green and Blue". This symbolises the flexibility, or plasticity, of individuals in different settings. It also symbolises the process of getting to know the Others, from a stranger to a person that we know in more depth. In the beginning you see easily the colour preference, which is the first stereotyping. Then you see the text and can read about the other preferences, too. Then you are in the advanced stereotyping mode (Bird et al., 2000). Then later you come to know and see different aspects of the Other in greater depth beyond these categories. This is the process where Others become individuals, and the concept of Others is being constantly revised based upon personal experiences with individuals belonging to another group.

Flexibility is not only about personal choices. Different situations invite different types of role behaviour, either because it is natural or smart. There are tasks that are naturally Blue, like quality control, proofreading, gathering data etc. There are times when Blue behaviour is recommended, like for example at the end of the week where closure of tasks is important for a good weekend without work. Sometimes Red communicative behaviour is essential in service complaints, involving people etc. And, sometimes seeing new opportunities with a Green attitude is the only way out of a difficult situation. It can be a smart move, for instance to start re-analysing the overall situation when conflicts among partners escalate instead of resorting to emotional conflict management. A smart move might be to suggest a new idea for a Green leader when decisions have been made, introducing the idea of analysing potential gains of different strategies to overcome hurdles that might come. A smart move towards Red might be to involve everyone in the harvesting of data for analysis of a critical situation instead of making a fast and "wise" decision.

Sometimes we also are caught up in the social dynamics. Sometimes joining with the team, other times disagreeing in order to show distance. "I disagree with you. I am not like you." When we differentiate, we show our uniqueness. When we join, we show that we belong. Life is very often a dialectical back-and-forth in these positions. Allowing disagreement without expelling the person that voices disagreement is important in order to have a viable and creative internal dynamics in the team or organisation. Expelling people who disagree becomes a signal of punishment for voicing different perspectives. As long as the disagreement is not in major conflict with important underlying

Figure 2.2 Green, Red and Blue badges

values and goals, the acceptance and exploration of diverse ideas is a way of cultivating constructive dialogues that lead to better discourses and debates.

Voicing is easier in a culture of acceptance. Are there any of the coloured groups that disagree more often than others? Yes, Green people seem to be a bit more individualistic and alternative thinkers. At the same time, they seek positive feedback on their excellent ideas. That is not always easy to satisfy. I sometimes say that "If Green suggest a very good idea early in the morning, and has not received any kind of acknowledgement before lunch, they send their resignation before the end of the day!"

Sometimes people work in working cultures that are dominated by one colour. Taking a contrasting role in order to position a dynamic polarisation might be a good thing. If you live in a very creative oriented organisation with little success of implementation, you might ask yourself if you have enough Blue qualities to take that role in this setting. Even though you are naturally very Green. Playing the "Devil's Advocate" is a way of taking a role position that contrasts the main cultural dominance. The "Devil's Advocate" is for challenging the position by taking the opposition role. In Red, Blue and Green diversification we see people take on different roles to fulfil what they see as needed. This is sometimes named as the "law of requisite variety" in some cultural theories.[5]

From self-insight to meeting Others

Now I have described qualities of people with preferences in Red, Blue and Green dimensions. Knowing yourself as well as knowing how the Others are different, are essential elements in any interaction between people whose basic assumptions diverge. Red, Blue and Green have different preferences for how they prefer to be met and to take this into consideration will increase the possibility of getting the message through. This was the original project of creating Red, Blue and Green as communicative strategies in 1995. In the guidance for engineers at that time we used these guidelines partly inspired by Dick McCann's book on interaction at work place (McCann, 1988).

Guide to communication with Others

How to succeed with goal oriented communication? When the guidelines for engineers were made in 1995 for how to effectively approach customers with different colour preferences, we applied an adaption of the guidelines that Dick McCann used in his book on work life interaction (McCann, 1988). The guidelines looked like the following.

Red preferences:
  Use conversation, harmonious discussion
  Be personal and enthusiastic

Focus on social consequences and community spirit
Show trust and consideration

Blue preferences:
Give them time for reflection and consideration
Be down to earth, practical, focus on usefulness
Be logical, goal oriented
Use facts and examples
Focus on details
Use numbers and calculations
Be structured and well prepared

Green preferences:
Focus on higher ideas, the larger picture and connections
Be positive to change and future possibilities, visionary
Be open to creative and innovative ideas
Set high goals
Be value-oriented

When we trained the engineers in 1995 we focused upon what they should do in different stages through the communication with the customer. First of all, we asked them to give positive complements to the customer that came and asked about advice. Asking for advice as a customer is a position where you yourself do not know the answer and you assume that the engineer does know. This is a situation where engineers feel pleased by being acknowledged as experts and encouraged to immediately show off their best and most relevant information. We recommended that before giving any advice, the engineers should first positively acknowledge the customer for being a competent advice seeker. This changes the focus from information on energy conservation to the customer as a person that is taking initiative in establishing a potentially valuable relation.

We then asked the engineer to work with the customer to map the challenges of energy consumption from the customer's perspective. At the same time, we trained them to listen for the elements in the customer's understanding and communication that could indicate their Red, Blue and Green preferences. Following this mapping, we guided the engineers to find solutions that first of all were relevant from the customer side as well as phrased in the preferred Red, Blue or Green forms. We then suggested that the engineers complement the customer for listening and for their willingness to take action at home. They followed up by sending information to the individual customer confirming the recommendations given. In this follow up letter, a sentence was added to the end introducing three additional pages: "If you want to do even better, and know more about how Others have been initiating activities in order to reduce energy, look at the next three pages." One of the pages was Red and that exemplified examples of how Red people often did changes in energy conservation, a Blue paper with typically Blue changes, and a Green paper with possible Green changes.

Being an advice seeker is normally a position where the adviser stands out with her/his expertise. In our personal history we all have multiple experiences listening to parents, teachers and professors where we feel immature and uneducated. The design of this interaction was meant to be a contrast to this feeling of incompetence. This process was meant to build a positive self-image for the customer as being competent in advice seeking as well as a successful energy conservation customer.

An integrated colourful person

In psychology, we often find the distinctions between feelings, thinking and behaviour – and in many folklore, educational and change models you find Head, Heart and Hands/Body (Scharmer & Kaufer, 2013) with the idea that you need to develop all three to be fully integrated and whole. In my approach with Red, Blue and Green I have had a special focus on individual differences and how they play out in the interaction between people. When we measured Red, Blue and Green preferences, we focused on the first preference, and compared this with the others in interaction or in the team. Almost every person has distinct first, second and third preferences. How should an individual understand and approach all their three preferences?

Human Dynamics is a movement created by Seagal and Horne (1997) over two decades ago where they presented an interactive model based on their three chosen principles, Emotional, Physical and Mental. Their conception of how these principles interact adds some useful thinking on how an individual's preferences for Red, Blue and Green may interact internally. Seagal and Horne suggested that the strongest preference has a core centring and forming function, while the second preference adds content. The third preference they suggest is the one that can challenge the individual for personal development. So, to summarise, they suggest that the first principle (in our case, the strongest preference for either Red, Blue or Green) sets the centre and form, the second adds content and the third is the one that can challenge you in your personal growth. There are some small differences in content between the Human Dynamics model and Red, Blue and Green. But, the structure of the dynamics in between the three categories points out a direction for internal development. How can this dynamic model be applied to Red, Blue and Green?

Let me take myself as an example. I have Green as my first preference, Red as the second and Blue as the third. This would imply the following.

First preference Green: I connect ideas, look for the larger picture and I am triggered by new ideas with wide ranging potentials. I am spontaneous and flexible. My energy is stimulated by new ideas and new experiences. In my enthusiasm I can be dominant due to strong values and interpersonal energy. I am willing to consider almost any possibility and often develop multiple solutions to a problem. I move quickly from one project to another.

But, with Red as an added preference: I also connect with people, not only ideas. I am open to see and respect Other perspectives. The interpersonal side of Red softens me a bit, such that I can be friendly and expressive as well as innovative in the social arena. I can be flexible not only in mind, but also in behaviour and in relation to Others.

And with Blue as a challenge for development? Blue is a challenge. What missed opportunities are there as consequences of less attention to the Blue direction? What potential for growth is there by taking more care of Blue perspectives? Perhaps I could be more consistent in following up initiatives and through such consistency increase trust in my capability of leading change. I might be overbooked by opportunities and commitments, and thus need to take time for reflection and contemplation. I have to be careful not to overlook logical, factual realities when making decisions. I can easily see opportunities, but might be "blinded by the light" of future possibilities. I should spend more time analysing limitations and use my creative brain with Others to re-examine decisions and overcome hurdles. Risk analysis might be a good collective activity to establish a more realistic plan.

This model implies that I am able to relate to all three preferences in myself. With this model I can focus on personal development in an integrated way with Red, Blue and Green. With an awareness of all three colours there is a possibility of individual development through introspection and reflection.

Case: Third preference challenges

In a leadership developmental program we made groups of leaders based upon first and second preferences, and asked them to define a challenge based upon their third preference. The following are the results from the group work.

- Red-Green challenge: Be precise in decision making and follow up.
- Red-Blue challenge: Be courageous and future oriented.
- Green-Red challenge: Stepwise and anchored processes.
- Green-Blue: Take time to involve people.
- Blue-Red: Do not avoid conflicts and discussions.
- Blue-Green: Listen, acknowledge the need of social processes.

An integrated awareness of all three colours will also make it easier to recognise with empathy the Others, independent of their level of Red, Blue and Green. Mentalisation, seeing things from the Other's perspective and reconciling with the Other's qualities becomes easier. In this way the language of Red, Blue and Green adds an inclusive aspect beyond interacting well with each Other based upon each Other's strength. More of this will come in Chapter 9 on the creation of an inclusive community.

A Scandinavian cultural component

As I mentioned in the first chapter, Diversity Icebreaker evolved from a Norwegian context. And, due to Geert Hofstede's recommendation, I think it is important to consider how much the cultural context has created some contextual qualities that have emphasised some things as important or not (Hofstede, 2001). In Scandinavia there is cultural quality described by an author named Aksel Sandemose, formed as a ten points law in one his novels (Sandemose, 1933). The overall theme is. *You are not to think you're anyone special or that you're better than us.* The law's function is to make everybody alike, no one stands out as being better than the Others. Positive self-expression is absolutely not aligned with this rule. The growth of Diversity Icebreaker as a concept in Norway is a cultural reinforcement of elements in the society that moves in the other direction. A Viking-law has been suggested as an alternative during the last years. *Know that you are unique* – is one of the sentences in this law.

I am not sure how this cultural background can explain why and how the Diversity Icebreaker concept has grown out of a Scandinavian context. But, I think it is worth mentioning. The Diversity Icebreaker process makes people stand out as being different, but they are not alone in being different; being different is part of an inclusive whole. Being different, but not alone in being different makes a huge distinction

A Norwegian post-doctoral student took part in a mentoring program. She was extremely high on Green. She said. *"I have never ever in my academic life felt included. This is the first time I feel that I belong – because I am together with a group of Greens. And we have so much in common. And we are one third".*

Summary and learning points

In this chapter I have introduced the deep level diversity categories of Red, Blue and Green. I have treated them as psychological categories relevant for diversified communication. I have pointed out the potentials of learning from each Other, both to see the Other person from their perspective as well as learn about self from the Other due to their outsider and observer position. At the end I have internalised the three colours into an integrated perspective of self-development. This chapter has only briefly described the classical Diversity Icebreaker seminar, a seminar that makes it possible to reflect upon more advanced theoretical perspectives. The next chapters will bring this perspective forward both with more thorough theoretical perspectives of communication as well as the potential of reflexive processes.

Notes

1 Global Diversity & Inclusion Benchmark is a standard for evaluating different organisational practices around different diversity issues. It has been developed with a join
effort from almost 100 experts since 2006. This definition is taken from their third
revision made in 2016. In this revision the UN Sustainability Goals are integrated and
as such move the ambition beyond compliance, social justice, competence, organisational development and dignity.
2 See, for example, https://www.aarweb.org/publications/rsn-may-2014-on-diversity-
institutional-whiteness-and-its-will-for-change.
3 In 1997 I delivered my MBA dissertation at Henley Management School in London
where I described the redesigned market communication and consultative follow up. I
estimated the value of reduced energy consumption at three levels; telephone interviews
of 100 customers reporting what they had done, an estimation based upon implementation of technical devices, and a comparison at county level of the electricity consumption.
4 In each box: What I see but you do not. What I see and do you, too. What I do not
see, but you do. What neither of us sees.
5 "The requisite variety condition"; see Thompson, Wildavsky & Ellis, 1990.

Bibliography

Anderson, N.R. & West, M.A. (1994). *Team Climate Inventory: Manual and User's Guide.*
Windsor, Berkshire, UK: NFER-Nelson

Arieli, S., Rubel-Lifshitz, T., Elster, A., Sagiv, L. & Ekelund, B.Z. (2018). Psychological
Safety, Group Diversity and Creativity. Israel Organizational Behavior Conference, 3
January 2018. Tel-Aviv, Israel

Belbin, R.M. (1981). *Management Teams.* London: Heinemann

Bloom, H. (2002). Can the United States export diversity? *Across the Board,* March/
April: 47–52

Bird, A., Osland, J., Delano, J. & Jacob, M. (2000). Beyond sophisticated stereotyping:
Cultural sensemaking in context. *Academy of Management Executive,* 14(1): 65–79

Costa Jr., P.T. & McCrae, R.R. (1992). *NEO PI-R: Professional Manual.* Odessa, Florida: Psychological Assessment Resources

Dept of Finance (2013). Stortingsmelding 12, 2012–2013. Perspektivmeldingen. https://
www.regjeringen.no/no/dokumenter/meld-st-12-20122013/id714050/

Edmondson, A. (1999). Psychological safety and learning behavior in work teams.
Administrative Science Quarterly, 44(2)(June): 350–383

Ekelund, B.Z. (1997). The application of a model which integrates market segmentation
and psychological theories to change energy consumption in households. Dissertation
MBA. Henley Management College/Brunel University

Ekelund, B.Z. & Jørstad, K. (1998). *Team Climate Inventory: An Intervention Manual.*
Oslo, Norway: Human Factors AS

Ekelund, B.Z. & Langvik, E. (2006). Team roles as Diversity Icebreaker. London conference
presentation: SIETAR: Society of International Education, Training and Research.

Ekelund, B.Z. & Langvik, E. (Eds.) (2008). *Diversity Icebreaker: How to Manage Diversity
Processes.* Oslo: Human Factors Publishing.

Ekelund, B.Z. & Pluta, P. (Eds.) (2015). *Diversity Icebreaker II. Further Perspectives.* Oslo:
Human Factors Publishing

Ekelund, B.Z. & PlutaP. (2017). Reframing Others in colors of mastery. Nordic Intercultural Communication, Conference, 23 Nov. 2017. Jyväskylä, Finland

Ekelund, B.Z. & Rydningen, M. (2008). *Diversity Icebreaker: Personal Workbook*. Oslo: Human Factors Publishing

Ekelund, S.M., Brannen, M.Y., Brannen, N.C. & Ekelund, B.Z. (2015). A trajectory theory of language development in organizations following Diversity Icebreaker seminars. Presentation. European Association of Work and Organisational Psychology (EAWOP), 23 May 2015. Oslo

Furnham, A., Steele, H. & Pendleton, D. (1993). A psychometric assessment of the Belbin Team-Role Self Perception Inventory. *Journal of Occupational and Organizational Psychology*, 66: 245–257

Grant, A.M. (2013). Rethinking the extraverted sales ideal: The Ambivert Advantage. *Psychological Science*, 24(6): 1024–1030

Hegge, T.I. (1997). *Rapport om arbeidet med segmenter, utprøving av kommunikasjonsbiter rød, blå og grønn og utprøving av kWh-kur*. Rapport til Akershus Eneriverk

Hofstede, G. (2001). *Culture's Consequences*. Second edition. Thousand Oaks: Sage.

Honneth, A. (1995). *The Struggle for Recognition. The Moral Grammar of Social Conflicts*. Cambridge: Polity Press

Jones, E.E. & Nisbett, R.E. (1972). The actors and observer: Divergent perspectives of the causes of behavior. *Journal of Personality and Social Psychology*, 27(2): 79–94

Luft, J. & Ingham, H. (1955). The Johari window, a graphic model of interpersonal awareness. Proceedings of the western training laboratory in group development. Los Angeles: University of California

Lane, H., Mendenhall, M., Maznevski, M.L. & McNett, J. (2004). *Handbook of Global Management. A Guide to Managing Complexity*. MA: Blackwell Publishing

Løvlie-Schibbye, A.L. (1983). *The Self*. Oslo: Universitetsforlaget

Løvlie-Schibbye, A.L. (1985). *The Self of the Psychotherapist*. Oslo: Universitetsforlaget

Margerison, C. & McCann, D. (1991). *Team Management. Practical Approaches*. London: Mercury Books

Maznevski, M.L. & Ekelund, B.Z. (2004). Cultural dimensions in action: Democratic elections in post-war Bosnia. *Organisational Theory and Practice; Scandinavian Journal of Organisational Psychology*, 1

McCann, D. (1988). *How to Influence Others at Work*. London: Heinemann.

O'Hare, J. & Richter, A. (2017). *Global Diversity & Inclusion Benchmarks*. Standards for Organizations around the World. Centre for Global Inclusion. http://centreforgloba linclusion.org/

Sabharwal, M. (2014). Is diversity management sufficient. Organisational inclusion to further performance. Public Personnel Management, 19 February 2014. https://doi. org/10.1177/0091026014522202

Sandemose, A. (1933). *En flyktning krysser sitt spor*. Oslo: Tiden. English title: *A Fugitive Crosses His Track*.

Scharmer, C.O. & Kaufer, K. (2013). *Leading from the Emerging Future. From Ego-System to Eco-System Economics*. San Francisco: Berret-Koehler

Seagal, S. & Horne, D. (1997). *Human Dynamics: A New Framework for Understanding People and Realizing the Potential in Our Organizations*. Arcadia, CA: Pegasus Communications

Stoltenberg, J. (2013). Speech. 8 March 2013, with reference to Dept of Finance. http s://www.tv2.no/a/3727388/

Strauss, A. & Corbin, J. (1990). *Basics of Qualitative Research*. London: Sage

Thompson, M., Wildavsky, A. & Ellis, R. (1990). *Cultural Theory*. Colorado: Westview Press

Van Gundy, A.B. (1981). *Techniques of Structured Problem Solving*. New York: Van Nostrand Reinhold

3 Communication models

Since 2013 a group of researchers at Hebrew University in Jerusalem have been running different experimental trials of the effect of the Diversity Icebreaker seminar. Tammy Rubel-Lifschitz is one of these researchers. And she commented in one of our research workshops that the way that the three colours of Red, Blue and Green play out in the room does not elicit power differences. In reality, power differences are almost always an issue. She thought that this was one of the reasons why participants found the seminar attractive. For me it becomes a reminder of how the Diversity Icebreaker constitutes an experiential space with psychological safety, different from the reality outside the seminar. It made me aware of my classical training in communication where power is a part of the context.

Introduction

In this chapter I will introduce different theoretical perspectives on communication that I find relevant when communicating well with the Other. I will start with describing the challenge of meeting Others. I will then gradually build the complexity of communication with Aristotle's rhetorics and his differentiation between ethos, logos and pathos which has some similarities to Red, Blue and Green. I will elaborate the Sender–Receiver model which has been central in many Scandinavian writers like Arne Næss, Ragnar Rommetvedt and Rolv Mikkel Blakar. I will expand the Sender–Receiver model with systemic and contextual perspectives. This is especially important for cross-cultural communication. Dialogue will be contrasted in relation to discourse and debate. The systemic family therapy tradition led by Tom Andersen in North-Norway with models of reflecting teams has added perspectives on the use of observer position. This leads into the concept of trialogue that I have introduced as a special form of three-way communication. Trialogue is the next step after monologue and dialogue. I will end the chapter with reflections on ethical norms for communicative practice – a practice that can inspire and guide personal and collective competence development. Central authors in this last part are Habermas, Hartmann and Benhabib.

Why do we communicate?

We do not see similarities, we see differences.

(Bateson, 1972)

I don't see myself as you see me, but is that a problem?

(Eckert et al., 2010)

Terje Hartmann wrote a book in 1982 on the conflicts of perception. In this book, he suggests that one of the reasons why we communicate as human beings is because we perceive things differently and we need to explore the fact that "I think you do not see things the way I do". He presents a theoretical model that provides good reasons for communicating beyond the more classical argument that we communicate for evolutionary survival. He states that it is this perceived assumption of difference that motivates us to communicate with Others. Then he adds on the idea that the motivation in this communication is often the aspiration that the Other will change his mind to align with one's own view. This is a conflict-reducing strategy where the assumption is that "I know better, and you should agree or subordinate". Theoretically Hartmann gives arguments for this solution of the conflict by referring to cognitive dissonance theory (Festinger, 1957) and Heider's assumption that people are attracted to people that are like themselves (Heider, 1958). Both are theories that focus on the uncomfortable situation of not being together with people that share similar qualities. Perceptions of differences seem to trigger action.

In Terje Hartmann's ideas about reactions to differences we find similarities to what we see in the conflicts between tribes where survival is essential. Protection of the tribe with "fight or flight" is the normal reaction. Throughout the history of man there might be a relative strong biological tendency for this behaviour. In our now highly networked global world with Grand challenges, we will systematically meet people who see the world differently from ourselves. And it is unthinkable that we will be able to solve these problems if "fight or flight" is our primary and only response pattern. In my point of view, it might be natural for human beings to act like this, but it is definitely not the most powerful problem-solving approach nor culturally attractive solution. I think we should advocate ideas that represent positive ideals for treating each other with respect. Fighting against Others' views as an instinctive response might be natural, but definitely it is not what I think is culturally attractive these days.

Mastering communicating with Others

"When I am together with people with the same mindset as myself – I do not need to say something. We just do things – and everything moves on in a beautiful flow. It is absolutely great."

This statement is typical for participants reflecting on learning points at the end of Diversity Icebreaker seminars. It refers to the stage in the seminar where they have been grouped in mono-coloured groups. And it contrasts the feeling of working and communicating with groups where colours are mixed, or where the norms, values and basic assumptions are not shared. In multi-coloured settings, uncertainty can occur when the reactions are not as expected. You meet a stranger. You meet an Other; you are faced with difference. What kind of difference is difficult to know. Do we think and understand issues differently? And if so, are you right or am I wrong? Do we value things differently? And if so, who will win in any conflicting value process? Do I and the Other perceive the world differently? And if so, how do we map out these different ways in order to create a shared understanding? The first question invites discussion, the second is an invitation to debate and the third is an invitation to engage in a dialogue. These can be seen as three different ways of engaging with the other, or "language games".[1] Do you and the Other know which of these language games is the best fit? Do you both know how to act in a way that will create mastery for both of you to succeed? Of course, most people cannot answer yes to these questions. And perhaps you feel ashamed of a lack of competence. For this reason, a feeling of uncertainty and discomfort can grow inside each of you. An easy way out is to leave the situation, or to not take part in any communication and remain silent. This is an escape route, and does not create anything new.

Another approach is to engage and fight for your own perspective. A third way would be to start talking and inquiring into each Other's worldview in order to learn, see and then act. This last exploratory approach of having a shared dialogue is what I recommend. This approach has elements of acting with dignity and respect towards the Other. This book is designed to give you more functional strategies of inquiry and co-exploration in uncertain situations.

Moving beyond rhetorics, discussion, debate and monologue towards dialogue and trialogue

In practice as facilitators, consultants and leaders, we live in a professional culture where dialogue is seen as the most valuable form of communication. It is a way of communicating, where respect for the Others and individual growth is central. Nevertheless, it is important to know and master other forms of spoken communication and recognise their unique qualities and potential applications. I will explore rhetorics, discussions and debates before delving deeply into the evolved Sender–Receiver model that underlies good dialogue.

Rhetorics

The Greek philosopher Aristotle (1954) focused on three different ways of getting a message across; ethos, logos and pathos. Pathos is about creating feelings and engagement. Logos is about giving good and rational arguments.

Ethos is about overall values and ethics. In his recommendations, he advised people to start with logos where you give good and truthful arguments that logically make sense. Then you strengthen the message by giving good ethical reasons. At the end, you add pathos in order to make things really happen with dedication and energy. Rhetorics presented in this way, is about how you can communicate effectively *to* Others. It is a monologue perspective where the ways of arguing are set up in sequence in order to have most effect on the Other. It was a teacher and pupil relationship, an unbalanced situation where one person knows better than the Other. There are no words or concern that consider taking into account that the Other person may have diverse preferences concerning what they find important in the communication or how they might perceive things differently because they have a different worldview. Aristotle's rhetorics does not take the quality of the Other into consideration. Such a model is good for marketing or lectures inside the same culture, but less suitable for dialogues where people need to find solutions that include differences in values, knowledge and background.

Case: Rhetorics training of leaders in hospitals

The first time rhetorics was directly related to Red, Blue and Green was in 2002 when one of the major hospital organisations in Norway applied the test of Red, Blue and Green in their leadership training. The participants scored themselves and trained to communicate with the participants with other preferences. In their training manual written by Marianne Synnes Kaasa (2002) they positioned Blue preference close to Logos, Red to Pathos and Green to Ethos. The training was meant as a self-awareness exercise as well as communicating with the Other in mind. Later on in this chapter I will introduce how Ragnar Rommetvedt has elaborated the psychological processes of how people being aware of the Other's differences leads to a change in communicative acts.

Discussion

In a discussion the idea is to seek the ultimate truth. Information is gathered and statements are tested as being either right or wrong. This is a communicative practice that is precise and relevant. It belongs to the traditions of the science of the real world. It is this tradition that makes the "real" world move forward with technical innovations making people's lives easier. The focus is on identifying faults; searching for what to confirm, refute or revise are the central principles driving knowledge creation. The dialogic practice of warmth, empathy and seeing things from the Other's perspective is not the pivotal criteria for success. However, this is not a question of either/or, or which is best. Both are excellent communicative practices as long as they are applied in the relevant setting for the right purpose and outcome. It is important that those involved have a shared understanding of the intentions and ideals that rule these different language games. As a leader you can be a role model in both forms, as well as being clear with people when different norms rule. This will reduce misunderstandings between people. As a leader, make clear distinctions between dialogues and discussions and be very explicit when decisions are made in order to invite everyone to move on to the next step.

In most academic institutions discussion is the most central form of communication. This probably works well in relation to the growth of knowledge in academic fields. Many people have experienced the academic work climate among colleagues being formed by the ideals of discussion, and not the practice of dialogue. For this reason, university employed academics are probably not the best role models in order to improve dialogic practice and attitudes. The lack of dialogical practice in academia can make these careers less attractive for quite a few people. Seen from outside, there is a huge difference between academic discussion, where the confrontation through published articles is used to drive knowledge forward and the contrasting practice of dialogue where exchanging views with empathy and willingness to explore leads to revision and integration of ideas and reflections from a higher perspective. These are at least two of the different ways of creating new knowledge.

Debate

Debate is a communication form that has grown from within traditional politics. In a debate the winner is the one who recruits the most people to vote for his/her standpoint. This will often lead to situations where alternatives are contextualised in a way that favour one side in contrast to the other. Rhetorics is also often a part of the political training that leads to success. Politics is also the place where values are contrasted for competition, dilemmas should be highlighted, and decisions made in order to make the most number of people happy with the result. Polarised values and taking a position of disagreeing with the Other is the form that makes it easier for us to see the difference. This makes it easier to vote for or against.

Organisations are political systems. By this I mean that leaders also make decisions where values are the central elements contrasting different alternatives. In business though, dialogue rather than debate, is more likely to lead to other types of solutions where win-win solutions can make the outcome more attractive for all involved. For these reasons it is recommended to have a good dialogue before engaging in political discussions.

Sender–Receiver model: the basis of good dialogue

The sender–receiver model is based on the idea that people receive information differently, and that this is something to be considered when choosing the best communication strategies. This idea was an essential element of the work by Ragnar Rommetvedt in Norway (Rommetvedt, 1972). He pointed out that we *encode* our own language based upon how we expect the Other to *decode*. When we constructed Red, Blue and Green in 1995, the idea was to apply three different communication strategies at the same time, in parallel, not as a sequence. Our idea was that the receiver had a preference for a certain type of communication and picked the one that made most sense from his or her perspective. The message was encoded in three different forms based upon the idea that there were three different but aligned decoding forms. We thought that an encoding that was aligned with the receiver's preference for decoding would increase acceptance and involvement. Once this effective communication was established, the joint solutions that included the Other's values and perceived opportunities and goals could be found. We took it for granted that people had different preferences and that this needed to be taken into consideration in any communication.

Seeing Others as different in a broader conceptual context

Arne Næss was a central figure in Norwegian philosophical discussions the first part of the 20th century (Sørbø, 2002). Through his lectures and books, he formed the curriculum for introductory university courses after the Second World War (Næss, 1947). He also established the field of eco-philosophy worldwide through his influential book on deep ecology in 1976 (Næss, 1976). In this chapter, I will focus on his contribution to communication training through his introductory courses at the university. In Chapter 9, I will follow up on his contribution to deep ecology based on how he positions humankind in nature.

In his lectures and books for the Norwegian universities. Arne Næss structured his examples in the following way: "Person 1 states sentence A to person 2. What are the different alternative ways that person 2 could interpret what person 1 meant to say?" In his books, he explores multiple numbers of situations, contexts, historical background and intentions that have a significant impact on which interpretation is more probable than others. Generations of students were trained to be aware of "seeing things from the Other's point of reference", or "in their shoes" as many people phrase it. It was established as a truth that you cannot understand the intention and meaning of a communicative act if you use your own reference point as the basic premise. Besides forming this general societal attitude through his contributions to university training, with these questions, Arne Næss also inspired the development of theories and practices in psycho-linguistic and communication theory. The Sender–Receiver model was then extended by Ragnar Rommetvedt (1972) and Rolv Mikkel Blakar (1984) in different ways.

The nature of interaction between physical reality and language is, philosophically, a very important exploration. Each one of us engages in the back-and-forth between language and reality in our everyday living and communication. To explore this dynamic beyond encoding and decoding, Ragnar Rommetvedt, explored the meaning of words and utterances by using a visual mapping which he called the "Semantic/nomological Network". During his university classes, he would position a word like, "thief", in the centre of a blackboard and invite students to come up and write associations to the given word. Sometimes we as students suggested words with similar meaning, sometimes contrasting meaning, possible relevant contexts, emotional connections and more. When we all stepped back to look at the result, we could see how we had jointly created a nomological network that created a deeper more contextualised meaning to the word/utterance in the centre. The overall drawing represented the way in which we as a group of students created a meaningful collective representation of the word. We saw very clearly that the word sometimes referred to something that was real, but we also saw that the context of associations created a broader way of showing meaning. It was a way of creating an additional linguistic universe to the word's reference function.

"A stone is a stone, because it is a stone. But, it is also a stone because it is not water." This statement was made by another philosopher, Jan Smedslund[2] in 1983, while he and I were sitting on the lawn discussing the reference function (essence) of a word. He had just picked up the stone in question off the ground outside the University psychology department in Oslo. He added the meaningful contrasts as an added perspective. "Something is, because it is. But something is, also because it is not." This is a statement that highlights and includes negation as a creator of meaning. In fact, the philosopher Saussure may have been one of the first philosophers to point out that negation and the network of context is part of the creation of meaning (Culler, 1976). At that time, Ludwig Wittgenstein also concluded that using words would never precisely describe reality, because the reference point and ensuing linguistic practice around the word and sentences would form the actual meaning of the description (Wittgenstein, 1922[1918]). Hence the ongoing dance between language and our perception of physical reality. *"As long as communication goes on, life is worth living". This truism was voiced by* Viggo Rossvær[3] as he discussed Wittgenstein with me in 1987. He shared how Wittgenstein had introduced the concept of "language game" in his philosophical foundations (Wittgenstein, 1953), published the year after his death. This is the background and meaning of this term which I use throughout this book. It is the basis of the dynamic interaction between language and physical reality.

The Diversity Icebreaker seminar has been directly influenced by these explorations above, where the meaning of a word is created by adding ideas for greater reference or contrast. In the classical Diversity Icebreaker seminar, after the questionnaire, the participants collectively write down what they associate with the categories of Red, Blue and Green within their three separate preference groups. As Reds, Blues or Greens, they draw together a broad description of each category, practising a form of semantic network mapping. They also co-create contrasting descriptions within and between Red, Blue and Green. In such a way, greater meaning is added to the categories through negation, what they are not. For example, if Red tends to be extrovert, Blues tend not to be. Extrovert Red behaviour defines Blue behaviour as introvert. These philosophical positions of "seeing in context" and "seeing from the Other's perspective" are essential parts of the Diversity Icebreaker seminar.

Your map is not like my map, but I did not know

Rolv Mikkel Blakar, is another psychologist who then took the Sender–Receiver Context Model into different experimental designs and further developed the theory. His work stresses the importance of our image of the Other as a premise for our own communicative acts. This is a very important contribution in order to understand why we choose particular words and communicative strategies towards Others.

Case: Communication

Two persons talk together; Ralph and Marie. Ralph the sender, wants to send some information to Marie, the receiver. Ralph will choose words based upon what he thinks Marie will understand. If she is a child, it is obvious that more simple language is chosen when investments are explained. If Marie is a lawyer, a more precise and elaborated coding will take place. Ralph "encodes" based upon his belief of what Marie is most likely to "decode".

But, Marie as an accountant might assume that Ralph has some personal interest of getting a buy in from the lawyer, and for this reason Marie assumes that some of the wording Ralph uses reflects an inflated over-positive judgement of the investment. Marie then decodes the message due to her perceptions of Ralph's motive.

As a consequence, being aware of the Others has implications for encoding and decoding.

In his much copied experimental design, Rolv Mikkel Blakar lets two people sit at tables either side of a thin wall, making it impossible for them to see each other while they communicate across the wall. Then one of the participants gets a map, for example a maze where a line is drawn. This first participant is then told that the other has a map, but the line is not drawn on the other's map. The map owner with the line is asked to give instructions to the other in a way that makes it possible for him to draw the line. Neither of them are told that the two maps are different. For example, the map for the receiver of instructions could be half the size. Then in different experiments, there are different rules for the communication; sometimes only one-way communication, sometimes the receiver is restricted to only saying "Yes" or "No" or sometimes, it can be an open dialogue where both parts can start questioning.

One of the interesting moments is when the instructions being given for drawing the line takes the line outside of the maze. Things are not turning out as each participant was expecting. This is the "moment of surprise". What is their reaction? Is it curiosity, frustration or maybe blaming the faulty sender or receiver? How and when do they realise that there is nothing wrong with the instructions, the fault is in the map? This is an exercise that cannot be solved without realising that each person has his own maze, his own map or his own worldview. When it is applied in, for example, cross-cultural training, its purpose is to create awareness of different worldviews, how to recognise and master the moment of surprise and then learning to craft questions in a way which make it possible to explore each Other's worldview. This is a central competence in cultural intelligence, a concept that I will introduce more thoroughly in Chapter 6.

A central learning point in the above exercise is that the world looks different from different perspectives and positions. Worldview differences emerge not only because of different perspectives, but also because people have different preferences, values, goals, norms, basic assumptions and histories – just to mention some of the many sources for worldview 'collisions'.

Metacommunication

Another important element is non-verbal communication which includes all aspects of body language, such as tone of voice, stance, gestures, facial expression, and physical comfort zones. The word was coined by Gregory Bateson in the 1950s (Bateson, 1972). Sometimes the overall "metacommunication" can strengthen the verbal communication. It can also represent an underlying message that has implications for how the spoken words could be understood. For example, when there are conflicts between verbal and non-verbal behaviour, the non-verbal behaviour will most often be taken for granted to be the most truthful. As a consequence, the verbal statement will be understood as a half-truth, sarcasm or even a lie. Non-verbal communication seems to function as a qualifier of verbal communication, a message about the message. It can lead to cross-cultural misunderstanding and even mistrust when sometimes quite different, even contradictory physical gestures accompany the same words, such as shaking one's heads from side to side to "I agree".

Power differences

Power differences often seem to influence the way messages are perceived when two or more people are communicating. Watzlawick et al. (1967) pointed out that power differences have implications for how important messages are perceived between the communicating partners. An example: If an expert states the fact or if a leader points the direction, the communicative acts are normally taken more seriously than made by a speaker who does not have the same level of expertise or authority.

If we summarise the theoretical perspectives mentioned above, from Næss, Rommetvedt, Blakar, Bateson and Watzlawick, we see four elements that are central to communicating with words in a Sender–Receiver model.

1   The sender often encodes the communicative acts based on expectations of how the Other will decode.
2   Metacommunication is likely to qualify how the stated words are understood.

3   Differences in perceived power usually influence the importance the utterances are given by the receiver.
4   Between communicative actors, words as well as sentences are perceived and attributed meaning within a specific context. If the context shifts, the meaning changes. Context creates meaning, both in reality and in the language per se.

Awareness of metacommunication and power differences are important elements in communication training. The context as the overall premise for the construction of meaning is important for both specific words, communicative acts and objects of reality. The context is systematically different for people from different cultures. Lack of awareness of the Other's cultural context can lead to blind misunderstandings. I will focus more on cultural context as an important premise for understanding in Chapter 6.

The move beyond monologue, discussion and debate to dialogue

Monologue

A monologue is the least complex form of giving and receiving information from another. If you do not ask questions, it is like a listening to a written text. Even though it is not an advanced communication form, it is an important way of sharing information, especially explicit knowledge for instructions etc. As mentioned above, if you know a lot about the Other and his/her context you might, as a sender, be better at encoding the message in a way that the receiver accurately decodes the message.

Dialogue

Different from discussion and debate described above, in a dialogue the focus is to adjust and elaborate the form and content of the message based on a reciprocal understanding between the communicators. You can ask for feedback to ensure that the information has been correctly received. Revising assumptions on both sides is a part of the game. Perspectives shift. William Isaacs (2008) refers to dialogue as "a conversation with a centre not sides" and explores four key skills of listening, respecting, suspending and voicing and how to put them into action balancing advocacy with inquiry and avoiding structural traps within a contained field of dialogue and conversation. "The heart of a dialogue is a simple but profound capacity to listen. As we explore, we discover listening is an expansive activity, giving us a way to perceive more directly the ways we participate with the world around us" (Isaacs, 2008). Isaacs goes on to point out that listening means not only to Others but also to ourselves and our own reactions. As such, in good dialogue, you learn both about yourself and about the Other, as well as about the Other person's point of view on the issue you are both concerned about. Dialogue can result in self-reflection, a revision of your own ideas of the Other as well as a more precise knowledge and understanding of the Other person.

Dialogue is the form of communication that promotes the qualities needed to master meeting with Others. In practicing dialogue, you often see a sincere will to understand the Other empathically. This might lead to more explicit understanding and communication about emotions and implicit and tacit knowledge. Personal reflection about your own preconceptions before meeting with Other's perceptions, value and worldview, can lead to revising your own basic assumptions and predefined attitudes not only of the Other, but also about yourself. Good dialogues make it possible to move beyond our more ordinary understanding of the ways we often categorise Others, like immigrants, economists, Greens and more. Dialogue demands a considerate will to bring forward ideas, listen and to ask more questions in order to promote each other's self-knowledge. This leads to a better understanding and openness for change for both people involved.

Trialogue

Trialogue is a concept which we have introduced in our practice. What is trialogue? First of all, it builds on the same good communicative practice as we see in dialogues. The open communication, sharing perspectives as well as willingness to revise one's own ideas and basic assumptions. However, in "trialogue" three people are involved. And the three people should not only be involved with dialogues in between each Other, but also use the third position to observe and give feedback on the interaction between the two Others. The system of three units is one system where one person actively reflecting on the interaction between the Other two is part of the whole system. In other words, the third person is not a neutral person but a systemic point of departure in sharing reflections about the interaction between the Other two.

Since both senders and receivers are actors in the interaction, they cannot observe themselves. As an observer of the dialogue between the Other two, you *can* observe the patterns of interaction in a way that those engaged in the dialogue are unable to do. This is the added quality that trialogue brings to the game. We know from attribution psychology that actors and observers see things systematically differently (Jones & Nisbett, 1972). Adding an observer creates the possibility of seeing and learning about the patterns of interaction in a new way.

Added to that, reflexivity, the ability to reflect on one's own behaviour and experience and adapt and change, is an important executive function of being a human being. We are able to reflect on what we see and hear happening in between Others as well as reflect on our own reflections. This practice of reflecting on how we perceive interactions has enormous potential to bring about change. We can describe these processes as naming, framing and reframing.

In multiple professional traditions you see the same structure of reflecting on the categorisation of the world, the naming in a framing. A conscious effort of reframing happens when something named is changed to a new name. Blue economists can focus on costs inside an annual budget, but a long term Green strategist may name the same money as being spent as an investment. You can easily see how the change in naming leads to a different perspective. Reframing might be to choose to explore economic implications beyond a fiscal year perspective in a five year horizon. More about naming, framing and reframing will come in the next chapter.

We can see an example inside theories of self-development by Anne-Lise Løvlie-Schibbye (1983, 1985, 2009). She says that self-development emerges as a consequence of reflecting on the interaction between self and observed self, self and the Others, and then reflective practice of seeing the interaction between these two interactions: "What do I learn about myself when I act aggressively towards Others? Could an alternative way of seeing the Other (reframing) elicit another interaction and learning?"

In cultural competence models of Cultural Intelligence, meta-cognition is coined as a central executive cognitive function for change and learning (Thomas et al., 2008). In sociology, one of the main sociologists in Norway, Hans Skjervheim (1959, 1976), is best known for differentiating between being a participant and being an observer. The observing position made it possible to reflect and share these reflections with those people who had been an object for study. By sharing this knowledge with those studied, the actors could integrate this new learning. The expected consequence is that this will ultimately change them and their view of themselves and then also the society will change.

With this new self-knowledge, the empowering question for these people that have been studied is "Now that we have some new knowledge, what can we do differently, given what we know?" In the literature on management teams, reflexivity is one of the main functions that distinguishes innovative and high performing teams (West, 2000; Ekelund, 2009).

The right to free speech –and your responsibility for giving the Other this opportunity

I started this third chapter with a focus on perceived differences, being aware of the differences, and different two-way communication processes, rhetorics, discussion, debate and monologues. I then explored how the Sender–Receiver models are deeply embedded within generative communication, which sits at the interface between language and physical reality and which can lead to dialogue and joint problem solving where everyone's ideas are integrated into a synergistic solution. I continue with interaction forms that include reflexive observers with multiple actors involved, leading to change and new ways of interacting. Interactions where the focus is on engaging with the process and co-creating a joint conversation which evolves from moving on from each person's starting position. For sure the power of the argument and the power of taking a position is relevant in many contexts in discourses and organisations where decisions are taken. However, in community settings and in democratic societies the norms of taking part in communication are different than in science and business organisations.

If we are deeply convinced that democracy is a highly esteemed societal quality, then we need to act in a way that promotes processes that makes it easy and positive for everyone to take part. Making knowledge accessible and creating arenas for discussions, debates and dialogues are important. Important too, is to create a climate where people feel free to voice (Habermas, 1981). When there are differences in power, knowledge and competence in knowing how and when to interact and communicate, there is a need to proactively overcome these differences and make sure that less privileged people and groups are supported to take part in democratic processes. At the political and institutional level, this is what we see in Affirmative Action in the USA, and in the rule of having at least 40% women at the boards of public listed companies in Norway. At an individual level it is a question of mastering different methods for facilitation and communication across these differences.

Although there has not been a major international armed conflict for 70 years, we are seeing a fast growing world-wide ecological crisis. Violence and armed conflicts between different groups, sometimes based on ethnic differences, religious differences or fights over degraded environments and complex interactions between different factors continue to create climate and conflict refugees. These are crises and conflicts that neither the country's political system nor global actors have yet been able to solve. People crossing borders versus the right to inherited land for those born and raised within a nation leads to challenges for liberal and wealthy nations. How do we solve these migration issues at the same time as we hold dear the ideas of and functionality of democracy and national control? How do we let people into our civil societies? Will nation states and the control of land and who has access to the political and socio-economic systems continue as the most pertinent boundaries for democratic systems?

The ecological crisis we see emerging taking place in polluted air and water, with rising CO_2 concentrations and resulting land, air and ocean temperatures, is a potential accelerator of change. Neither air, water, heat, nor ocean borne plastic pollution respect national borders. Global agreements are imperative in solving the problems. Can we collaborate to act quickly enough to avoid serious negative changes?

I am afraid that we will be challenged on democratic processes both inside and between nations. We will be tested as to whether we can solve these challenges at the same time as we promote dignity and inclusion in social interaction. Technology will of course be a part of this solution, and technological problems will be solved by people interacting between scientific disciplines. Both consumer and producer behaviour needs to change and both information campaigns and economic incentives will drive these changes. It is my hope that we will be able to solve these problems with many people involved at the same time and be able to keep up the democratic practices in a European tradition. China's one child policy, its investment and growth of renewable energy worldwide are examples of speedy and effective ecological problem solving without democracy as an integral part. At the same time, it is unclear what the impact of the parallel growing need for wood, coal, oil, and mineral resources is having in Africa for instance. By swapping building infrastructure for resources, many African countries are becoming increasingly indebted without adding value to their own extracted resources at the national level. Can democracies act fast enough?

In Western Europe we have developed a democracy where we show respect for minority positions and their interests. We have a welfare society were the aim is that the sick, elderly and underprivileged have access to some minimal standards of support to meet their basic needs. We have some ideas that have historically emerged from the Reformation, times of "Enlightenment" and the "Renaissance", namely that individuals and certain institutions, such as the media, have rights and freedoms and there is a belief in the benefit of all citizens sharing knowledge. The competence to communicate with Others in order to solve problems and create better interaction is a relatively technical competence. In order to solve the challenges we have ahead, I have found it helpful to build my own dreams and visions aligned with social philosophers like Jürgen Habermas (1981), Axel Honneth (1995) and Martha Nussbaum (2016). One of the thinkers who has highlighted the democratic challenges of today very precisely is Seyla Benhabib. In her book *Dignity in Adversity. Human Rights in Troubled Times* (2011) she discusses the ethical challenges in communicative interaction and rationality. She states that if freedom and democracy is the overall wish, and there are differences in power, the people in power have a special responsibility to make sure that the voice of the Others is heard and respected. My intention is that this book can help to build this competence among people in power to influence problem solving in relation to the global ecological crisis, involving people from all over the world.

In this chapter I have focused upon different communicative models and theories relevant for communicating with Others. Ethos, logos and pathos have similarities with Red, Blue and Green and historically anchored the concepts. Different communicative language games are presented and the differences of their nature presented in order to underline that communication is not only a dialogue where the importance is to see things from the Other's perspective. The context and power dynamics are elements that are important to address in order to understand the Other's view and communicative behaviour. This is especially important in order to reinforce Others' freedom to voice. In the next chapter I will elaborate how communication and reflexivity can lead to learning processes. The concept of trialogue will be further contextualised based upon my personal history with developing the practice of reflecting teams in family therapy.

Summary and learning points

1   The challenge is to communicate with people whose basic assumptions and preferences for communication are different from your own.
2   Rhetorics is a one-way communicative strategy to share information with the Other.
3   The Sender–Receiver model accentuates the need for the sender to encode their communication according to their expectation and understanding of how the Other will decode. Knowledge of the Other is the premise for the encoding.
4   Every communicative act has a content, a metacommunication and happens within a power structure and a specific context. Context, power and metacommunication strongly influences how the content will be perceived and judged.
5   Discussion, debate and dialogue have different rules of the game and different goals and outcomes. To master all three, and knowing when each of the different forms is best employed, is an individual competence as well as important for participants to agree on in order to communicate effectively.
6   The reflexivity process has significant potential in societal processes and politics. If we want democracy to rule, we have to makes sure that each individual feels free to voice without being punished. This includes also asking questions in relation to political governance systems in a global world.
7   Reflexivity is a key for alternative perspectives that might trigger better solutions, dreams and engagement.

Notes

1   A term coined by Ludwig Wittgenstein in 1953 to describe the interaction between language patterns and reality.
2   Jan Smedslund was engaged as a professor at Psychology Department at University of Oslo. He was a professor with a dedication to logic and common sense understanding.
3   Viggo Rossvær was engaged as philosopher at University of Tromsø, Norway. Inspired by Ludwig Wittgenstein he spent lots of time with Tom Andersen´s group of therapists in Northern Norway, expanding perspectives of the application of language in therapy, systemic thinking and the practice of Reflecting Teams.

Bibliography

Aristotle (1954). *The Nicomachean Ethics of Aristotle.* London: Oxford University Press
Bateson, G. (1972). *Steps to an Ecology of Mind.* New York: Ballantine Books
Benhabib, S. (2011). *Dignity in Adversity. Human Rights in Troubled Times.* Cambridge, MA: Polity Press
Blakar, R.M. (1984). *Communication: A Social Perspective on Clinical Issues.* Oslo: Universitetsforlaget

Culler, J. (1976). *Saussure*. Glasgow: Fontana/Collins

Eckert, R., Ekelund, B.Z., Gentry, W.A. & Dawson, J. (2010) Rating discrepancy in 360-degree feedback: "I don't see me like you see me, but is that a problem?" *European Journal of Work and Organizational Psychology* 19(3): 259–278

Ekelund, B.Z. (2009). Cultural perspectives on team consultation in Scandinavia: Experiences and eflections. *Scandinavian Journal of Organizational Psychology* (2): 31–40

Festinger, L. (1957). *A Theory of Cognitive Dissonance*. Stanford, CA: Stanford University Press

Habermas, J. (1981). *Theorie des Kommunikativen Handels. Band I und II*. Frankfurt am Main: Suhrkamp

Hartmann, T. (1982). *Opplevelseskonflikter*. Oslo: Universitetsforlaget

Heider, F. (1958). *The Psychology of Interpersonal Relations*. New York: Wiley

Honneth, A. (1995). *The Struggle for Recognition. The Moral Grammar of Social Conflicts*. Cambridge: Polity Press

Isaacs, W. (2008). *Dialogue. The art of Thinking Together*. New York: Crown Publishing Group

Jones, E.E. & Nisbett, R.E. (1972). The actors and observer: Divergent perspectives of the causes of behavior. *Journal of Personality and Social Psychology*, 27(2): 79–94

Løvlie-Schibbye, A.L. (1983). *The Self*. Oslo: Universitetsforlaget

Løvlie-Schibbye, A.L. (1985). *The Self of the Psychotherapist*. Oslo: Universitetsforlaget

Løvlie-Schibbye, A.L. (2009). *Relasjoner*. Oslo: Universitetsforlaget

Nussbaum, M.C. (2016). *Not for Profit. Why Democracy Needs the Humanities*. New Jersey: Princeton University Press

Næss, A. (1947). *En del elementære logiske emner*. Oslo: Universitetsforlaget

Næss, A. (1976). *Økologi, samfunn og livsstil*. Oslo: Universitetsforlaget. Translated into English (1990) *Ecology, Community and Lifestyle: Outline of an Ecosophy*. Cambridge: Cambridge University Press

Rommetvedt, R. (1972). *Språk, tanke og kommunikasjon: ei innføring i språkpsykologi og psykolingvistikk*. Oslo: Universitetsforlaget

Sivertsen, M.V., Ekelund, B.Z. & Esnault, M. (2004). *Social Democratic Leadership; Team, Leadership and Projects*, Oslo: AOF

Skjervheim, H. (1959). *Objectivism and the Study of Man*. Mag. Degree, University of Oslo

Skjervheim, H. (1976). *Deltakar og tilskodar og andre essays*. Oslo: Aschehoug

Synnes Kaasa, M. (2002). *Leadership Training in Helse Øst*. Internal Training Manual. In Norwegian.

Sørbø, J.I. (2002). *Hans Skjervheim – en intellektuell biografi*. Oslo: Det norske samlaget

Thomas, D.C., Ekelund, B.Z. et al. (2008). Cultural intelligence: Domain and assessment. *International Journal of Cross Cultural Management*, 8(2): 123–143

Watzlawick, P., Bavelas, J.B. & Jackson, D.D. (1967). *Pragmatics of Human Communication: A Study of Interactional Patterns, Pathologies, and Paradoxes*. New York: Norton

West, M.A. (2000). Reflexivity, revolution, and innovation in work teams. In: Beyerlein, M., Johnson, D.A. & Beyerlein, S.T. (Eds.), *Product Development Teams: Advances in Interdisciplinary Studies of Work Teams* (pp. 1–29). Stamford, Connecticut: JAI Press

Wittgenstein, L. (1922). *Tractatus Logicus-Philosophicus*. New York: Harcourt Brace & Company

Wittgenstein, L. (1953). *Philosophical Investigations*. London: Wiley-Blackwell

4 On the power of reflexivity

There is a story being told among family therapists in Norway. It is probably not completely true. But, it is a good one and it goes like this.[1]

It was in one of the rural communities in Northern Norway, beyond the arctic circle, where a family therapy session was taking place with therapeutic professionals from Tromsø as facilitators. Traditionally, the set up involved experts (the reflective team) behind a one-way screen and a therapist as the interviewer in the room with the family and the family's important others.

In one session, the microphones between the therapy room and the observers' room did not work. The experts asked if they could sit in a distant corner of the room as they could no longer hear in the room behind the one-way screen. The family said "Yes, you can". When the experts wanted to discuss their ideas on what they had observed, they found it uncomfortable to keep this dialogue to themselves. After all, the family had been open with their internal dialogues. So, the experts decided to exchange ideas and share reflections in the same room while the families were listening to them. They then shared their resulting conclusive instructions. Observing the next round of communication between the family members, the experts realised that their instructions were being ignored. Nevertheless, they witnessed that each of the family members had picked up on different elements of their reflections from their observations and applied them to themselves in relevant and positive ways. In sum, all the family members integrated initial communicative elements − but not the expert's overall concluding instructions.

Reflexivity in family therapy from Italy to Tromsø

This episode is a story that is shared among family therapists to describe a pivotal narrative in the transformation of practices in family therapy. I was a member of this Tromsø group for three years in 1984–6, and for me, this story highlights the most important eye-opener of the potential power of using reflexivity in a non-expert way, in relation to Others, in interaction. There were lots of professionals involved in this work, but most important and most often cited was Tom Andersen (Andersen, 1987). I will present this experience more thoroughly before diving into the power of reflexivity as applied at different points of the Diversity Icebreaker training.

In the family therapy tradition, an Italian group developed a systemic approach where a group of experts were observing the therapist interacting with families. Sometimes the therapists were working in pairs and sometimes the families were invited with their network of important others (Selvini Palazolli et al., 1978). The therapists were one system, the families and network another system, the group of experts another system – and then, these three systems in the room were also seen as a larger system.

In the Italian tradition, the experts observed from behind a one-way screen; discussed the interaction between the therapists and the families between themselves and finally gave instructions to the therapists and families. Their focus was on the interaction and creating changes in the interaction, not on the qualities of individuals. The language they applied was a language of processes and change. When the expert instructions were given, the idea was that the expert's advice would make it impossible to continue the interaction that kept family members locked in unhealthy patterns. The instructions given were aimed at inserting a new power structure. The family participants could use the momentum of this opportunity to act in a different way. New initiatives were often seen, resulting in more functional behaviour from many of the members in the family.

In Northern Norway, Tom Andersen and his colleagues were inspired by this practice. They created a large training and learning practice that had the most powerful impact on family therapy in Scandinavian countries. The reflecting team approach (Andersen, 1987) gradually evolved from the traditional family therapy traditions in Italy (Selvini Palazolli et al., 1978) as well as in the USA (Minuchin, 1974) where some uniquely different approaches were developed.

Multiple voices within the expert's system created multiple communicative elements, where each family member picked up on what they found relevant and helpful in their stuck situation. The experts reflected back on their original way of working and decided to forget the one-way screen and leave out the idea of any concluding instructions. Instead, they would keep on exchanging different perspectives with multiple voices while the families were listening all the time in the same room. Importantly, the experts kept their observations focused on interaction patterns, processes of change and ways of using language that did not stigmatize individuals with more rigid qualities. In the process, the families evolved from families taking instructions to individuals picking elements they each found helpful. The individuals in the families had turned into actors in their own life. The group of "expert" observers that functioned in this way was called "the reflecting team"[2] and has become a major part of many change processes, not only in family therapy, but also later on in organisational change and supervisory practices.

The experience of Tom Andersen and his group is a manifest illustration of using the observer position to reflect on the interaction between Others, to work uniquely with multiple voices and to recognise the potential of change for individuals within the whole system. For me these group processes became an external manifestation of the internal reflexivity that has been an essential part for all liberating psychotherapeutic practices since Sigmund Freud's introduction of psychoanalysis. "Where Id was, there Ego shall be" was his maxim, indicating the strength of the Ego's reflective capacity for conscious change in relation to more deterministic and chaotic unconscious forces.

This model of family therapy with three sub systems within a whole system has elements in line with the theoretical perspectives underlying trialogue processes and the Diversity Icebreaker seminar presented above. It illustrates how each individual can reflect on themselves within interaction and consciously see and choose another way of seeing and acting. It is this individual choice that is illustrated in Anne-Lise Løvlie Schibbye's personal growth model mentioned in Chapter 3. It illustrates Michael West's concept of a team's reflexivity (West, 2000) where team members pause, reflect on what has happened, learn and then consistently act with the intention of making a change for the better. In sociology, you can find the same type of processes at a societal level in Hans Skjervheim's work on actors and observers and how the sharing of social science knowledge in a public discourse will lead to a change in what was being studied (Skjervheim, 1976).

Tom Andersen's family therapeutic practice added some elements inspired partly by constructivist systems theory of autopoiesis (Maturana & Varela, 1980). The idea is that each system, whether the system is an individual, family, group or organisation, self-creates its models of understanding through continuous ongoing reflexive processes. Maturana and Varela thought that it was impossible, from an external point or view, to create a control or change system that is not aligned with the way the system itself can accept control or change. Tom Andersen thought that each person and family will themselves choose the information they find relevant to build into their own future process. Others could not control this internalisation of Other's ideas.

For this reason, what the therapists or experts could do, at best, was to present lots of alternative ideas and voices without the idea that some were better than others. However, it also undermined the position of experts as experts and took away the ethical responsibility of being hired as an expert by a public funded health system. For me this was problematic and for this reason the underlying focus on ethics and implicit and explicit values has become very important in healthcare systems as well as in my work. Done well, multiple voices, shared reflections in many directions, if underlined with care and respect, can create a climate of information sharing that can generate lots of unforeseen creative actions. The focus on processes in between actors was very often a new naming, framing and re-framing. Everyone in the whole system creates a new framing in which to see themselves.

So this underlying ethical climate and the structure of having a third system for seeing and commenting on the interaction between two Other systems as a creative process is the structure that I wanted to highlight by using the name trialogue. You might say that in the Diversity Icebreaker process we break the ice, the participants un-stick what is stuck, and they bring into action the communication between three system groups. Sometimes we play with mono-coloured groups of Red, Blue and Green, and like in Tom Andersen's family therapy – each system has its own communication and dynamics. Sometimes we let all the colours be together, and create a larger system of interaction. We do not have one system that has the expert position, but the colourful groups share their observation of the Other as well as the interaction between themselves and Others. Since no one is an expert or has the right to define what is right and wrong, it becomes a process of sharing reflections to Others who are free to integrate learning due to their own openness for change.

Different levels of learning

In the Diversity Icebreaker seminar there are different levels and types of learning belonging to the different stages in the seminar. In the first stage, participants are engaged in a process of understanding themselves and Others. They apply the test as a way of mapping reality. This is a way of thinking we very often find in sciences were the focus is to understand the world, framed within natural science. In the second and third stage, the categories of Red, Blue and Green are socially constructed through dialogues in and between groups. This is a practice that represents social science. It is about the words and models we apply in the way we see the world. In the last stage we ask participants to reflect upon the practices in the first three stages. This last reflexive process about mapping the world (stage 1) and socially constructing the categories (stage 2 and 3) is a process that is central to the sciences within the humanities.

Homa Bhabha states that in the humanities we study how we as human beings create social systems and use different types of words to understand the world (Bhabha, 2011). The three scientific traditions, natural sciences, social sciences and humanities, are split into different faculties in most western universities. But, in the Diversity Icebreaker seminar we can see these three traditions being integrated within one process.

We start with a natural science model of mapping the world, the reality out there. We *name* personal qualities. Then we use this mapping as a stimulus into a social process of creating the meaning of the three categories. The questionnaire has been predefined and constructed to map inner qualities of Red, Blue and Green preferences in a valid and reliable way. When participants start to explore the categories that are relevant for themselves, they elaborate their understanding of their colour in their own context. They *frame* the categories. This is a social process of communication and agreement. In the last stage we ask questions to bring out the learning, including possibilities to see Other ways of naming and framing, so we can *re-frame*. But we can also frame and reframe the naming and framing, which in other words, is about what we understand about how we understand. Now, it starts to become complex. Now, we need examples and illustrations.

Examples of naming

Most participants start to explore their own scores by referring to how they see themselves in relation to the test-score. They talk about it in a way that is referring to an inner reality of themselves.

Here are examples from participants that belong to understanding the world of self, Others and the interaction:

- "I recognize my self being Blue."
- "Of course I, as a Blue person I find it challenging when Green come up with radical new ideas at the end of the project when we need to focus on the completion of the tasks."
- "I like Blue, because they are reliable."
- "I guess Blue is more functional in some stages, and Green in others. I cannot see how Red can contribute, so, that's a point that I have to learn more about."
- "It is difficult to state that one colour is better than the other, they have only different functions".

These statements refer to learning about the colour-categories in practice, referring to the world of description and action. Some comments refer to evaluative perspectives of good or bad, positive or negative – which very often is a part of reality as long as categories have implications for oneself and Others.

Who am I, really?

1. Questionnaire: Who am I?

Figure 4.1 Who am I, really?

Examples of framing

I think most individuals often reflect upon themselves. The Diversity Icebreaker process promotes these self-reflective processes to a greater extent than usual.

Elements of this reflexivity are about the categorical system and implicit qualities. Examples of this are:

- "The categories 'Diversify & Unify' at the same time."
- "It is strange how much we know about Others without knowing them."
- "My wife stopped being a problem when I understood she was Green."

The first statement refers to an understanding of the categories at two levels. The categories make distinctions. At the same time participants see that the qualities of any one colour only represent 1/3. The other colours are also needed. So, the categories make distinctions between people, they diversify, *but* at the same time they unify within an integrated whole.

The second statement refers to the participant's awareness of how using a colour label implies making assumptions about the Other that are not rooted in a history of directly knowing the Other person. While providing a potential entry point into getting to know more about the Other, biases may well occur through such a simplified labelling.

The last statement refers to the awareness that my perceiving my wife being troublesome is due to my own perception. It implies that "if I have another idea about my wife – my interaction with my wife will change".

The idea of Red, Blue and Green categories as an integrated whole, a Gestalt where the parts are defined by each other and in relation to the whole Gestalt, is a perspective illustrated by these citations from participants:

How do I see myself and the Others?

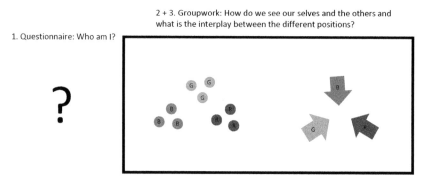

Figure 4.2 How do I see myself and the Others?

- "It seems that one colour is defined being different from the Others, like Yang-Yin."
- "It is good to be different if my uniqueness is needed by the Others."
- "Being acknowledged for who I am is important for me in my interaction with the group."
- "It is strange how fast and easy it is to become a group when we were labelled Red and started to work together."

The first statements refer to an element that is essential for integrating Red, Blue and Green perspectives, as well as integrating the people presenting such perspectives. Since the participants are involved in discussions where three categories are described, they very often map the world of communicative acts in opposing ways. The trilemma structure at the end can, for this reason, embed lots of active dilemmas, making it relevant to balance, integrate or drive these different perspectives for change – not to ignore them. This characteristic of the process of categorization, of creating dilemmas and tri-lemmas that need to move to an integrated resolution, seems to lead to a cognitively integrative but differentiated structure. This in turn, leads to the individual and collective reflection that is referred to in the second and third statement; that being different is ok if it is acknowledged by the Other. The fourth statement refers to the sociological processes of forming groups, with labelling as an added quality.

The important idea here is that it is the mental models and language we use that forms how we see and evaluate Others. It illustrates a linguistic perspective on the process of understanding the world. Argyris & Schön (1996) defined this perspective learning at level II. Level I is about reality, while level II is about the models we apply in order to understand the reality. In the family therapy mentioned above, we created situations where people could see and talk differently about themselves and Others. Very often, this is the central part of any therapeutic process. We do not change the world in therapeutic dialogues, but we change the way people see the world – and for this reason they can act differently.

In the real world, outside the room of therapy or the classical Diversity Icebreaker seminar, participants can ask "What language categories do we use? Do they describe the world adequately? Are they functional? Do they create beauty?[3] Shall we con-tinue to use these categories – or shall we create some new ones?" This empowers individuals and groups to take control of the power of language, and its implications in the world.

Examples of re-framing

Argyris & Schön added a third level of learning, level III, the level of learning about learning. How do we frame the framing and naming process? How do we set up processes where we learn about how we create categories that can be applied for describing the world? This perspective is only possible to do after a process of naming the world, and being aware that this naming process is inherently framed by ourselves because of the way we apply mental models in describing the reality. This perspective is possible in the last stage of the Diversity Icebreaker seminar, and can be illustrated graphically this way.

When we become aware that we see the world through our own senses and perceptual models, we also become aware that there must be other ways of framing. Different psychological tests represent alternative framings, and they are very often mentioned in Diversity Icebreaker seminars. Through these discussions, participants also become aware of how different the process of creating Red, Blue and Green is compared to traditional learning about for example introvert and extroverts. Traditional psychological concepts are something we acquire knowledge about through reading research and literature grounded in research. The classical Diversity Icebreaker seminar illustrates another type of learning because the participants themselves co-create the meaning of the colourful categories from what they already understand and can reflexively identify about themselves. The whole idea about establishing categories of individual qualities is re-framed though this alternative practice.

I have now introduced learning at three levels. Let me illustrate more clearly how the different ways of learning are connected with different scientific traditions and how they manifest in the Diversity Icebreaker seminar. I will start with level I, learning about reality through models from social sciences. Then level II will be illustrated with how we see categories emerge. On Level III I will also include elements of reflexivity the way it is being described in 2nd order science, radical constructivism, which is the philosophical tradition that fuelled the family therapy tradition in Tromsø.

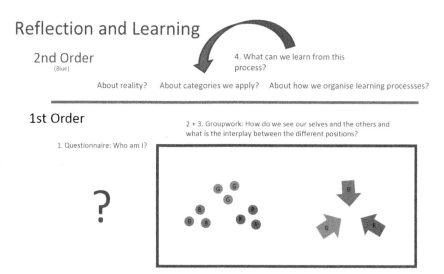

Figure 4.3 Reflection and learning

Level I: A psychological model of defining the reality of Red, Blue and Green

As shared above, the first stage of Diversity Icebreaker seminar looks like an execution of a classical positivistic psychological test. Reality should be described in a valid and reliable way. In our own studies aligned with these traditions, we have empirically validated that the dimensions measured in the questionnaire are formed by personality, values and cognitive styles (Ekelund & Pluta, 2015). Today we describe Red, Blue and Green as preferences for communication.

The nature of these validation studies is that they do not analyse one individual, the individual, precisely. Participants will find that the description embedded within each category is seldom a complete or fully accurate description of any one specific person. The inherent nature of these studies is to aggregate data from many individuals, and so the pattern of description (meaning Red, Blue and Green) of categories is correct when, at best, it describes the systematic and statistically significant variations within a large grouped database. In other words, personality categories emerge from the aggregated data of many individuals across particular ranges.

When we introduced Red, Blue and Green, we looked for similarities with such large data studies and our categories have indeed been confirmed in many studies. The patterns of Red, Blue and Green data have overlapped with established categories in for example personality categories, emotional intelligence, values etc. (Ekelund & Langvik, 2008; Ekelund & Pluta, 2015).

However, as suggested, the categories do not necessarily describe all individuals in an accurate way. Some people are more original in the way they have developed their identity. For these people, the categories from large data studies have limited potential to describe that individual. In order to describe these people, introspection and observer's feedback become more useful tools.

The usefulness of the categories that are embedded in the classical Diversity Icebreaker seminar is that they can in fact be tilted in a unique way for the individual, as well as for groups that have some special characteristics that make them unique. The active social construction of Red, Blue and Green by the participants themselves in the Diversity Icebreaker seminars is a way of opening up for specific and local and possibly more precise descriptions, pertinent to the people in the room.

Level II: The social creation of meaning or Red, Blue and Green

The creation of meaning in the classical Diversity Icebreaker seminar is only partially influenced by the mapping in the questionnaire, the tradition that dominates Agyris's level I learning. The co-creation of meaning within the categories in the second stage of the seminar does indeed build on the questionnaire items belonging to each colour, but more importantly, it also includes participants' personal experiences and insights that emerge from their active communication in each of the three mono-coloured groups. This process of active involvement in crafting the meaning of the individual categories from within the three groups seems to have the same effect as being fully involved in change management; it reduces "resistance to change". Participants rarely oppose what they themselves have created.

The process often triggers over-arching positive emotions that enable participants to share both negative and positive connotations about their own group and the Others. These positive group processes can also give them the licence to engage in political incorrectness, bragging about themselves while making negative statements about the Others. The feeling of uncertainty, shame and fear of being disowned when the results are presented, combined with the pride of being in a group of good similar people – creates a tension that is at its peak when each group presents the results to each other. Seeing the Others acting in the same way, mirroring their own process, makes each group reflect on their own and the Others' processes with both laughter and reconciliation. A learning point is that being open to both the positive and negative sides of oneself and the Others, is ok if those sides are shared within an integrative culture, with inherent mutual respect in psychological safety.

Actually the high level of humour in this process triggers self-reflection. Bergson (1911) stated that people who laugh can look at themselves from the outside, both capable of as well as practicing self-reflection. The classical Diversity Icebreaker seminar combines the seriousness of the natural science model of psychology; the test psychology tradition, with the playfulness of enjoying group processes, competiveness, and courage to say what you normally do not say, leading to social probing, yet the relief of all tension at the end. This combination of seriousness and playfulness is an important part of humour that stimulates learning. Humour that is not at Others' expense, functions as a classical and operant reinforcement of sharing insightful information in context of uncertainty and unknowns (Ekelund & Moe, 2017).

The involvement, the reconciliation of self and Others being both positive and negative and the humour are rarely talked about spontaneously by the participants. Yet for us as trainers in Human Factors, we have seen that these elements are relatively unique and we think they are central for the successful dissemination of the concept worldwide.

Radical Constructivism and 2nd order science – an added perspective on level II learning

Müller & Riegler (2014) address 2nd order science in "Radical Constructivism" as "the operation of re-entry", where the two motivations for engaging in 2nd order science are the inclusion of an observer and self-reflexivity. This allows 2nd order science to operate on the products of "normal" or 1st order science.

In Diversity Icebreaker the 1st order science rules when the colour categories are applied as descriptions of the inner quality of people, the real world. The way it is described in level 1 learning.

In the second stage of the seminar, self-reflexivity in the mono-coloured groups and reflecting about the Others become the main activities. These are processes of 2nd order science and lead to a change in the understanding of oneself and the Others through the reflexive processes.

If we combine these ways of learning with what we learned in the family therapy in Tromsø, in addition to understanding oneself and the Other, we can add in the focus on the interaction between the Others. The object of focus in family therapy is the interaction between actors, seen and reflected on by multiple observers. One of my ambitions with introducing trialogue as a communicative practice is the increased potential for more systemic change and learning by applying observers reflecting on the interaction of Others. The outsider perspective on this relationship seems to give opportunities for adding perspectives to the communicative processes. As actors themselves, the two involved parties in the communication cannot take such an outside perspective.

I asked myself "How can I design a learning process that builds on all these elements?" In 2013, I was given the task to reduce prejudices and increase respect and quality of communication between three organisational units with 60 participants. They were merged six years ago. The organisational units belonged in three different countries and represented different scientific traditions. One of the units produced products, the other designed the products and the third managed the whole organisation. Different levels of power were in play.

Case Agon: Trialoguing

a) The whole group was divided by the Red, Blue and Green colours in each of the national groups.

b) These small mono-coloured groups representing each of the countries discussed how they experienced challenges interacting with the other national sites.

c) Three large groups were then established. In these groups they all represented the same colour, but were mixed across nations. The idea behind having the multinational groups working together in one-colour groups was to establish a common ground across nations and functions with similarities in communication preferences. Each group comprised of participants of one colour and different nations (e.g. a group of Norwegians, Germans and Swedish with Red preference working together). The focus here was on how one nation perceives the Other, e.g. how the Germans perceive the Swedes. The third group, in this example the Norwegians, were to reflect upon what they had observed in the interaction unfolding between the Germans and the Swedes. In their observations and reflections, the Norwegians were asked to focus both on challenges they had seen in the interaction and smart interactive moves that could lead to progress.

Work in this phase was organised in three rounds. Here is an example of Round 1 in the mono-coloured group:

1   Germans present to Norwegians how they perceived challenges work-
    ing with them.
2   Norwegians present to Germans how they perceived challenges work-
    ing with them.
3   Norwegians and Germans engage in a dialogue.
4   Swedes have dialogues among themselves while the Norwegians and
    Germans observe. They dialogue on how they see and what they think
    about the interaction they have just witnessed; Norwegians and Ger-
    mans listen to their comments.
5   Norwegians and Germans reflect on the comments from the Swedish
    group and formulate learning points

The exercise above illustrates application of the ideas from the trialogue
where the similarities of colours are the basis of a common ground – using the
outsider's perspective on the interaction as a creative, add-on perspective.

Level III learning and the power of reflexivity in learning about learning

In Agyris's level III, the reflexivity is applied backwards in time. Everyone with
multiple voices is invited to reflect on the whole process. We know that the
process contains elements from level I, the description of people with ideas
about describing reality. It contains elements from level II, about the process of
setting categories and co-creating these with mono-coloured groups as actors
and observers of Others. And, level III components, like learning about how
such processes can be set up, learning about learning. In seminars we find that
both facilitators and participants ask questions like: "Can we analyse the
development of categories from other areas of diversities? Can we explore critical interactions by involving groups in the same way every month within this
organisation? The positive and negative comments we apply in the organisation
today, do they reflect similar types of processes in between groups?"

The collective reflections mentioned above represent an advanced collective
learning process. A capability of such dialogues and trialogues in the organisation will probably increase the robustness to manage complex problems. Grand
problems, problems that address everyone across the world in relation to
human and nature's survival, are complex problems that need some combination of simplicity in common ground and complexity in diversity of perspectives and competence. In Chapter 7 I present how individual ideas can
contribute through good communication to collective new solutions. In
Chapter 8 I describe efficiency ideals for diversified teams and underline that
collective reflection, the way it is described above, is an important part of self-
management of teams. In Chapter 9 I highlight the potential for involvement
of people in a dignified way by taking care of inclusive community, trust and

collective identity. These three chapters reflect different goals that all are important. The capability of managing different ways of communication described in Chapter 3, as well as capability of reflexivity described in this chapter, are important people processes in problem solving and decision-making. Through the application of reflexivity from an outsider position, observing systems of people in interaction, new types of knowledge will emerge. Although it is my view that the complexity of Grand and wicked problems needs competent people to try out different communicative and learning processes. Theoretically I will explore this in the future inspired by different 2nd order sciences models. But, we need also to practice and learn the different ways of running such processes now. My intention is to reinforce the application of these models in the years to come, addressing these complex issues. Examples of this are given in Chapter 10. But, before we address these chapters, issues of scientific paradigms and cultural differences needs to be presented. Global problem solving will be influenced by these diversities.

Summary and learning points

1   Level I, II and III highlight differences in learning that also reflects different traditions in science.
2   Reflexivity from an observer position on people in interaction gives an opportunity to see patterns that are not seen by the actors themselves. The actors see from their actor's position, which always will be different from that of the Other actors as well as the observers of actors. The position defines their entrance and ways of seeing.
3   Bringing observers' perspectives into the communication reframes the understanding of oneself through the communication. Very often this reframing is from a logical higher level; seeing the pattern of interaction between actors.
4   When we ask "What did you learn from this process?" in the classical Diversity Icebreaker seminar, we invite participants to reflect afterwards upon their experience. The last process might lead to radical changes in ways of organising learning.
5   Trialogue is a form where an additional observing position focuses on an interaction between two Other groups. Feedback from the observing position will often lead to unpredictable change.

Notes

1   Tom Andersen (1992) writes a story of this change that is much more rational with emerging ideas over years, but with an incident in one of our joint team therapy sessions in 1985 leading to this open reflective process.
2   The "reflecting" concept was used due to the Norwegian meaning, close to French meaning, "look upon again, rethink and return". Not like the English application of "replication or mirroring". The inspiration to name the process the Reflecting Team

comes from the humanistic therapeutic tradition of reflexivity and change. We saw this humanistic process as an internalised metaphor and we applied the metaphor as an external interaction between groups in the communicative systems.
3   These three questions reflect the classical "Truth, Good and Beauty", an Aristotelian broad ambition for knowledge creation. In a conference presentation in 2009 I stated that the categories of Red, Blue and Green, the way they develop in the classical Diversity Icebreaker seminar, is halfway precise, very functional and creates lots of joy. Later on, I have found the assessment to be better than halfway precise (Ekelund & Pluta, 2015).

Bibliography

Andersen, T. (1987). The Reflecting Team: Dialogue and meta-dialogue in clinical work. *Family Processes*, 26: 415–428

Andersen, T. (1992). Reflections on reflecting with families. In McNanee, S. & Gergen, K., *Therapy as a Social Construction* (pp. 54–68). London: Sage

Argyris, C. & Schöen, D.A. (1996). *Organizational Learning II: Theory, Method and Practice*. Reading, MA: Addison-Wesley

Bergson, H., (1911). *Laughter: An Essay on the Meaning of the Comic*, C. Brereton & F. Rothwell (trans.), London: Macmillan

Bhabha, H. (2011). Humanities a culture of knowledge. https://www.youtube.com/watch?v=tFXaaFUYxLA

Ekelund, B.Z. & Langvik, E. (Eds.) (2008). *Diversity Icebreaker: How to Manage Diversity Processes*. Oslo: Human Factors Publishing

Ekelund, B.Z. & Moe, T. (2017). *Innovation Booklet*. Oslo: Human Factors

Ekelund, B.Z. & Pluta, P. (Eds.) (2015). *Diversity Icebreaker II. Further Perspectives*. Oslo: Human Factors Publishing

Maturana, H. & Varela, F.J. (1980). *The Cognitive Process. Autopoiesis and Cognition: The Realization of the Living*. Berlin: Springer Science & Business Media

Minuchin, S. (1974). *Families and Family Therapy*. Cambridge, MA: Harvard University Press

Müller, K.H. & Riegler, A. (2014). A new course of action. *Radical Constructivism*, 10(1): 7

Pluta, P. (2015). Systematic use of humour in HR training concepts – An example of the Diversity Icebreaker. Paper presented at the 23rd Nordic Academy of Management Conference NFF 2015 – Business in Society, Copenhagen Business School, 12–14 August 2015

Selvini-Palazolli, M., Boscolo, L., Cecchin, G. & Prata, G. (1978). *Paradox and Counterparadox: A New Model in the Therapy of the Family in Schizophrenic Transaction*. New York: Jason Aronson

Skjervheim, H. (1976) *Deltakar og tilskodar og andre essays*. Oslo: Aschehoug

West, M.A. (2000). Reflexivity, revolution, and innovation in work teams. In: Beyerlein, M., Johnson, D.A. & Beyerlein, S.T. (Eds.), *Product Development Teams: Advances in Interdisciplinary Studies of Work Teams* (pp. 1–29). Stamford, CT: JAI Press

5 A deeper look at the scientific disciplines and professional cultures

Having covered Red, Blue and Green as the first type of deep level diversity in Chapter 2, let me start this dive into this second type with a personal story from my first experiences as a trained psychologist.

In my first position as a psychologist I was attached to a psychiatric ward with a social worker, medical doctor and a chief psychiatrist. The chief psychiatrist was from Egypt. He had worked as a doctor in the military and trained as a psychiatrist in UK before coming to Norway. His approach to team work was based upon a clear understanding of professional competence and we were given client tasks due to our unique competences. As a psychologist I was given tasks that fitted with my psychological competencies, and I delivered results I knew none of the others could do. My professional feeling of being competent increased by his trust in delegating the task. His authority was undisputed. He decided who was to do what and helped when needed. This was my first experience with teamwork.

We spent a few years together as a team before national level trade union conflicts invaded our local institution and our team was reorganised. The nurses wanted more influence at the ward level, advocating against the perceived over-directive medical authority in the psychiatric hospital system. Latent conflicts between psychologists and medical traditions were brought up again. Hospitals have been ruled by medical doctors for many centuries. However, there are few good reasons in the medical doctor's education that legitimise their capability of managing large organisations like hospitals. Questioning, testing and opposing authority is a part of every person's upbringing and every profession fights for status and legitimacy in society. I started to see that many professionals in teams in the health sector did not have the same positive experience as me, of being acknowledged professionally. Later on, I understood that the psychiatrist managed our team using a model of administrative split in his distribution of tasks.

Which differences most affect problem solving and communication?

I have presented Diversity Icebreaker and the deep level diversity of Red, Blue and Green in Chapter 2. The Diversity Icebreaker process is built on personality related differences that form preferences for interaction and communication when we solve problems together in groups. In this chapter, I will introduce a second type of deep level diversity that is created through education and professional practice. Paradigms are the shared basic assumptions and practices inside specific scientific disciplines. Different scientific disciplines and paradigms across a broad range of professional activities constitute core elements in the interdisciplinary challenge

This chapter will draw out some of the functional similarities that exist within all deep level diversity systems. One of the similarities is that deep level diversity often leads to surprising moments when meeting Others, and these surprising moments will have elements of basic assumptions in the language structure and for this reason are most often, partly unconscious. These diversities are also deeply intertwined with values and emotions. I was made aware of these similarities during my first face-to-face interaction with Martha Maznevski in 1997. It goes like this.

Early in my career, in 1991, I was trained in York, UK, by Dick McCann in the team role model that he had developed with Charles Margerison (1991). The team role model was an assessment based upon the classical dimensions of Carl Gustav Jung which you also can find in the Myers–Briggs Type Indicator. I spent years with hundreds of managers and workers in teams and departments in order to train them to see and over-come differences due to individual personality oriented qualities. I used this model when I worked with management teams which most often consisted of people representing different professional units within an organisation. I frequently saw that, for example, the financial controller, the HR manager and the head of Research & Development had different personality profiles. But, when they argued, I could see that the whole discipline they repre-sented also had qualities aligned with the individual differences. Sometimes I thought that their personality qualities had influenced their career choice, including having the legitimacy of being a leader in such divisions. It turns out, this is probably true at a certain level.

In 1997 I invited Martha Maznevski who was an expert on cross-cultural management, to a joint seminar. In her PhD thesis, she focused on manage-ment teams, but with the cultural differences as her topic of study (Maznevski, 1994). We spent days talking about the differences and similarities between the diversity categories of personality, professional paradigms and cultural values in the way we saw them emerge and play out in management teams. Ten years later we were able to synthesise this in a presentation at the Academy of Management annual meeting (Ekelund & Maznevski, 2008). We focused on four similarities all relevant to individual identity; differences are embedded in *language, values* and *emotions* are involved, and important elements of these diver-sities are *unconscious*. When you see that any action or behaviour evolves out of a mix of different expressions of these four elements, the intersectionality is high. It becomes difficult to discern exactly what is going on. All elements are core to the identity of the individual. Internal self-awareness as well as the ability to see the Others are important qualities that are needed to begin to sort them out.

In our presentation at the Academy of Management, we stated that these qualities were sticky and challenging to communicate about – and that running a Diversity Icebreaker seminar first can make it easier to communicate and explore these differences together. In the Diversity Icebreaker seminar participants experience language development through defining the colourful categories, identity development, a revealing of unconscious qualities and lots of emotions. Red, Blue and Green are relatively easy to grasp while scientific paradigms and cultural differences are much more sticky and complex. Most importantly, Red, Blue and Green are staged in a positive and trust-building way that makes it easier to further explore the more sticky elements of other diversities within the group. We shared the idea that the positive climate created will increase openness and sharing and that it is easier to delve into and discern the areas of diversities due to scientific disciplines and cultures when participants have first experienced the classical Diversity Icebreaker seminar and positively explored Red, Blue and Green at a shared personality and cognitive level.

The key features of the Diversity Icebreaker seminar that prepare groups to explore "sticky" differences are the following.

1   A psychological safe and positive atmosphere, a safe learning space is created.
2   The basic structure of Red, Blue and Green where categories are embedded in the language, partly unconsciousness, with values and emotions, are equally relevant when groups of people belonging to different scientific paradigms and departmental cultures apply their "tribe" language.
3   Seeing, recognising and knowing about the qualities and the development of Red, Blue and Green give the participants an easier entry to see and talk about ideas, values and models that are central to their own professional culture and knowledge.
4   This sharing of ideas between people from different professions with an increased awareness of their own professional culture will make it easier to understand and solve complex tasks where scientific knowledge is an important element in the solutions.

We also had a more general idea that the "easy-to-understand" seminar of Diversity Icebreaker could be applied as a pedagogical model to make a group of people understand how other diversities can be well managed. Then, the group could take this higher metaphorical and process learning from the Red, Blue and Green structure and explore and discern the more sticky areas where both surface and deep level diversities were involved.

As hinted at above, we do find that the different scientific and functional professional paradigms interplay with cognitive styles assessed in the DI questionnaires. In fact, given the complexity of the intersectionality, the boundary between personality, scientific approaches and culture is fuzzy. So I will focus next on describing the diversities within scientific disciplines and professional practices. In the next chapter I will dive into the cultural differences due to upbringing. Then the last chapter will bring all this together to look at how we can tackle the wicked Grand problems and do Good.

Education and professional practices: scientific disciplines as paradigms

Professional identity

What kind of basic conflicts are represented in the case from my first engagement that I described at the beginning of this chapter? At the individual level, it is a question of relationship to authority, a generic issue where we all have to find our own way including raising the next generation to take over authority. The relationship to people in power is described in personal development, management of organisations, as well as embedded in major cross-cultural differences. For professions there is a question of acknowledged expertise, rights and roles. For the individual as a professional it is a question of one's own self-confidence as well as professional identity in self-selected professional education.

At the same time, the professional identity for the individual is often established through the historical approaches to the professional education given by universities and promoted by trade unions. Both people from universities as well as the trade unions are more interested in promoting their field compared to facilitating local interdisciplinary teams. Yet, for the client of organisations, it is important that all professional people work together successfully as a team across organisational level and disciplines. In medical hospitals as well as airline crews, low quality of integrated teamwork can have a direct effect on mortality and quality of care (West et al., 2002).

As you can see, there are lots of elements that can be brought into analysing the core dimensions of functional and scientific differences and integrative processes if the ambition is to understand what is going on when problems emerge in interdisciplinary teams. In my work as an organisational consultant, I have spent lots of time discerning and identifying the motives and interests in conflict ridden situations in such interdisciplinary teams. I normally apply a psychological and historical understanding as the building blocks when I share my understanding of an issue for the team to explore. But, over the years I have shifted from this historical problem-oriented way of looking at the issue to a more solution oriented way of un-sticking the situation. Looking for opportunities is much more inspiring than looking backwards to pinpoint who thought who was responsible for what.

In the last 20 years there has been a growing interest in more future-oriented ways of working together to find solutions to difficult situations. There are two main reasons for this. Firstly, a solution oriented focus seems to easily trigger positive involvement and motivation. The problem oriented focused has the opposite effect. Secondly, in the evaluation of what is good, bad, right, wrong or functional, it is difficult to decide if something is good or bad if you do not have some ideals and norms as a standard. If you know how things should be, you can "learn from the future" and decide what to leave behind, continue or add on (Scharmer & Kaufer, 2013). But, do we have clear ideas about what the ideals are for interdisciplinary team work? In the case I mentioned above, our teamwork functioned as an administrative split. This is not the only way to work together across disciplines. There are some different basic forms for how good interaction can play out. To have a shared understanding and acceptance of the rules of the game for optimal interdisciplinary work is important for good interaction. Do most interdisciplinary teams have such a shared and aligned model for this type of teamwork? At least, my impression is that teams very often lack a general understanding of what possible basic forms there are to choose from. Without this knowledge, how is it possible to create this shared mental model that builds efficiency, innovation or inclusiveness? In my view, more knowledge of the basic forms with good dialogues, discussions and debates in the team will increase the team's probability for success. I will present more about these basic forms in Chapter 7.

On becoming a psychologist

In my youth I experienced that friends found it helpful to talk with me when they were in serious trouble. I was surprised and felt very positive about this contribution. I thought that this could be my mission in life, an important function and role. I decided to study psychology in order to become a competent person in helpful communication. At the University of Oslo, Norway, psychology was organised as a professional study with clinical psychology as a core defining element of the profession. We received the title "psychologist" that was legally defined and protected. Specific job opportunities were available exclusively for people with this type of psychology degree.

The discipline of psychology is relatively young. It emerged in 1887 with studies on perception in Germany and came to Norway in 1924 as practical test psychology. The professional study at University of Oslo started in the 1950s and by 1972 the title was legally protected. Both employees at the university as well as psychologists in the trade unions fought to strengthen the status of psychology in many institutions through promoting the unique competences that psychologists could bring to the health sector and other segments of work life. As students we were proud representatives of our own profession and the Others were defined as those we were fighting against, most of all the traditions and privileges of the medical schools. This fight for and against become our narrative. It became our identity.

What was our relationship to other professions? In spite of the main focus on psychology, we were asked to take courses in disciplines like neurology, physiology, sociology, anthropology and statistics. They were named "support disciplines" and their contribution was framed as "in what way could these disciplines help us succeed in our work?" This approach did not build any in-depth knowledge of the other disciplines' competence, values and potential contribution. We were not trained to develop an attitude of acknowledgement towards people in the other disciplines. In order to succeed in an academic career, which was the main ambition for most academics at that time, it was a good choice to deepen the research into a narrow area where one can become one of the few stars in the world. The path to elite global recognition was to focus discussions and growth in this narrow area where only a few could contribute at an equal level.

It was also just as important, not to write and dedicate time to an area where others know best. This career approach is not easy to combine with breadth, knowledge of the other disciplines and a dedication to interdisciplinary research and teaching. The university's function in society is the development and growth of a specific discipline. No other institution has the same opportunity for specialisation. Other institutions like applied research centres and introductory schools are places where interdisciplinarity can have a higher priority. The reward system and organisational discipline structure within a university is not made for promoting interdisciplinarity. As a consequence, university representatives are often not the most practised role models in forming interests and attitudes that make students positive and curious in the meetings, as well as acknowledging and integrating the contributions of people from other disciplines. Rather, they may have to un-learn a sometimes inflated and unrealistic self-image of their own discipline in comparison to others and adjust their own perceptions of self-worth. They may need to be trained to see their own contribution from the outside, from a broader and more overall understanding of contribution. And they may need to be trained in constructive ways to integrate Others' and their own contribution when seen from the Other's position, with the other's professional paradigms.

Paradigms

Thomas Kuhn (1970) described some changes in science as a consequence of paradigm shift. A paradigm is a structure of ground rules for a discipline. It is related to what is important to study, how we categorise what we see, what methods we use and how we decide what is right or wrong. People who share the same type of paradigms constitute a scientific paradigmatic group with their own journals, conferences and internal references. They act as a tribe of insiders. Kuhn postulated that science does not progress in a constant growth of knowledge. Rather, a new way of seeing and studying emerges, and this way is incommensurable with earlier practice. The new paradigms start to rule when scientists based in the old paradigm either adapt or retire and a new generation takes over. He described this as a scientific revolution.

Paradigms constitute the platform for any type of scientific discipline. We can use the concept of a paradigm when a scientific tradition is described with fundamental differences in what and how a group of researchers study, the language and methods being applied, combined with more or fewer criteria of who belongs and who does not. It is a sociological phenomenon where the specific way of doing science is central for defining the group. There are similarities to this concept of paradigm and the concept of worldview, "fundamental cognitive, affective, and evaluative presuppositions a group of people make about the nature of things, and which they use to order their lives" (Hiebert, 2008)." And, there are similarities in the way we describe differences between cultures.

So there are some significant challenges when professionals from different disciplines choose to co-operate. If the paradigm defines how you categorise what you see, the person from another paradigm will see something different. Not being cognisant that there are two different views and that both are valid, will easily lead to a situation where you look upon the Other as lacking competence, or even worse, a liar and deceiver. If the paradigms define what is in focus, then context, border and blind zones are defined by the focus. You see your own focus, and from this point you see the context and the border – but you do not see on the other side of the border, the blind zone. You may not see that those you are choosing to co-operate with have another focus, based upon even another definition of focus, as well as having different ideas of what the context is, where the border is, and what is behind the border.

Quite often people from different disciplines also build a strong identity with their profession in work situations. Positive values are also aligned to this identifying strongly with your professional identity. Being true to one's own paradigm is valued very positively as remaining true to your discipline and expertise and makes it difficult to understand Others' use of categories and language, to acknowledge the Other's values and to understand why they focus the way they do. This constitutes the challenge, how do you understand yet go beyond your own position and at the same time, integrate the Other's perspectives through communication. The communication models laid out in Chapter 3 demonstrate the importance of being able to see things from the Other's point of view.

In our universities, we have a tradition of three main disciplines with different paradigms, namely the faculties of natural science, social science and humanities. It is easy to see how they differ in the content of what they study. The methods they use are different, too. In natural science researchers want to know what is the true versus false description of the reality. In the technical part of natural science they are interested in what works. In social science they talk about hypotheses that with a certain degree of probability are true. In the humanities they ask questions about ethics, aesthetic and religion. These distinctions make the Diversity Ice-breaker seminar into an experiential exercise that can be applied to illustrate different theories of science. The seminar illustrates that all three paradigms are relevant in everyday life. We talk about things that are important for us (humanistic values), with Others that are interested in the same issue (social influence and agreement), and we talk about it because we want to do something that makes a change in the real world (which is the object of natural science).

Epistemic cultures

Karin Knorr Cetina introduces a concept that has some similarities to para-digm and cultures and which is relevant for professional practice, namely *epistemic cultures* (Knorr Cetina, 1999). Epistemology is a branch of philosophy that focuses on "the nature of knowledge, justification, and the rationality of belief". "Epistemic" cultures emerge when employees work together, share experiences and develop a common understanding of how people and tasks are perceived and understood. Attitudes, values and ideas of best practices are examples of areas where common understanding will constitute elements in the collective identity of people working together. Such epistemic cultures are often seen in organisations where organisational departments are split by functions.

For example:

- A service office will have a culture where accessibility, ability to listen, fairness and openness are important.
- An administrative department will focus on predictability, consistency, follow-up and documentation.
- The research and development departments are often eager to promote open communication, investigation, piloting and creativity.

Geert Hofstede did an analysis of an insurance company in Denmark and found significant differences concerning values between the different departments (Hofstede, 1998). One of the departments was responsible for sales and had a culture of positive communication, seeing opportunities in the future and willingness to satisfy the customer. Another department thought they were the people in the organisation that really knew the field of insurance and for this reason thought of themselves as the core compe-tence in the organisation. The last group were those who administratively organised the company and took care of profitability, reliable reporting and stability in routines. Geert Hofstede, most known for his cross-cultural analysis, described the same type of attitudes and communication challenges between these departments as he typically saw when people communicated across different nations and geographically bound cultures.

Cultures in different organisational departments and their driving logic

When Geert Hofstede described these cultures in the insurance organisation, they also aligned with three different perspectives on leadership described by numerous researchers and authors. Juha Arvonen and Göran Ekvall (1996) described these three dimensions as driving forces constantly in interplay. They historically positioned the three dimensions emerging from a combination of the task versus people orientation that dominated the leadership literature research in the late 1950s and 1960s combined with the change orientation that became a strategic necessity following the oil crisis in 1972. These three dimensions have similarities in the way we often see differences in the Red, Blue and Green mapping in between departments. In the administrative department and functions, we see a dominance of Blue. In the more market, sales, customer and client oriented departments we find more Red. And, in the professional staff we often see Green to a much larger degree. Professional staff are very often concerned about knowledge based innovation, sales people are interested in improving the offer to the customer, and administrative staff are concerned with precision and efficiency. This is the same tri-lemma structure that we find among other scholars.

Rebekka Stenberg (2000) writes about different organisational logics in psychosocial health units in Sweden, between political priorities and economic constraints versus professionals and their values, norms and idealistic preferences, versus users' needs and wishes. Tian Sørhaug (1996) describes the tri-lemmas between societal accountability, user needs and professional responsibility and ethics. In many organisations where these discernible groups exist, we see people experiencing attitudinal and communication challenges between the groups, negative labelling of the Others and conflicting interests in search for influence and power. The challenge is to integrate these conflicting views.

3 driving forces, epistemic cultures

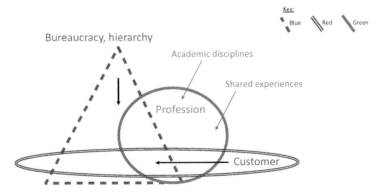

Figure 5.1 Driving forces and epistemic cultures

All three functions and the professional perspectives they each subscribe to are important to the total function of an organisation. It is not a good solution when one of the groups is dominating and ignoring the other group's perspectives. As a leader it might be fruitful to look upon these three perspectives as three driving forces that can move the organisation forward in creative interplay where ideas develop through creative friction. Through negotiations, integration and reflections on joint learning experiences, new perspectives might evolve across and within these three "epistemic cultures".

We often use this graphic to illustrate the colourful tri-lemmas. The professional Green dimension here is a combination of academic disciplines as well as "epistemic" cultures. Within organisations we often find these two perspectives of academic disciplines and epistemic cultures combined.

Forming cultures through categorisation

The interaction between reality and language has been a topic of huge interest in the humanities, as well as in psychology. The Sapir–Whorf hypothesis states that language forms perception (Whorf, 1956). At the same time, the content of perception is limited to our sensory capabilities. Language does not only have a referential function to the real world, language is also a social construction, revised and recreated by social and material interaction across generations (Schein, 1985). Language influences social interaction and becomes meaningful through actions and reflections. Even though language has a strong continuity, new words pop up representing a new phenomenon or a new perspective. #metoo is a concept that brought millions of people together in a joint speaking up process. It was an invitation to tell a story. And, when many people tell a similar story, it becomes a political power that suddenly reframes individual experiences. Heroes lose their fame, new norms emerge and #metoo becomes a symbol for the moment in history where men in power can no longer engage in sexist behaviour towards women. New words put into action change behaviour, norms and communicative interaction.

In the leadership literature, we find authors that focus on how the leader, through her or his views of the world, espoused through rhetorical communication, forms the employee's perception and attitudes. The leader wants the employee to focus on what she or he thinks are important areas in the organisation. This builds on the idea that the leader has the power to define and influence the employees through symbolic power via controlled communication (Alvesson, 1996). The leaders have the privilege to define the issue.

To introduce Red, Blue and Green as categories (models, metaphors) to characterise some inherently different qualities of customers and employees is an example of acts of power. As such, Red, Blue and Green can function as aligned leadership tools. In his theory of leadership, Erik Johnsen (1978) underlined the leader's responsibility as giving employees tools to facilitate discussions about goals and work flow processes. Language is such a tool. Implementing Red, Blue and Green as a frequently used organisational language implies that it can become a part of the organisational language and culture in a way that helps positively discern identities and open up perceptions and dialogue.

Three different scientific traditions behind the creation of Red, Blue and Green categories

In the Diversity Icebreaker seminar, the content of the Red, Blue and Green categories is constructed from within each group. In the seminar, you see elements from all three main academic paradigms mentioned above. When the participants start by answering the Diversity Icebreaker questionnaire as a psychological test, they are engaging in a psychological tradition of mapping internal values, preferences, attitudes as precisely as possible against validated categories. The idea is that the test result will be precise in referring to real personal qualities as if they were objective real world qualities. When they write about themselves in groups of the same colour, they pick out elements from the questionnaire that represent the "objective" quality from this psychological test tradition, an example of the natural science tradition. But, when they focus on elements and associations that are important to themselves, an introspective self-reflective process is brought out in the communication to the others in the same colour group. If you are in a Red group, you may hear "Reds seek harmony. Agree?" This internal process is a humanistic process of searching for the constructs of identity within a group of similars. When the others in the group agree or make changes in order to create a joint understanding, they illustrate the social negotiation of group identity, a process normally described in social science. When they share in the groups with the Others they illustrate the differences in perceptions that are normally described in actor–observer literature (Jones & Nisbett, 1972) and in the sociology of group labelling processes.

The content of what is written about each colour within each same colour group, when seen from inside and outside, is an integrated product of the initial questionnaire, personal experience and social agreement. It is the same three spheres of life that Habermas (1981) describes with his three different criteria for truth:

1   Is this a correct description of the world?
2   Is my story from within honest?
3   Between us, do we agree about what we see and say?

When we ask at the end of the seminar "What did you learn?", we invite each person and everybody together to reflect on elements of self-understanding, learning about Others, group dynamics, complementarity of the categories and eventually, the construction of language. This really is a humanistic turn which can be strengthened even more by asking the question "Based upon this learning, what kind of ideals can you formulate for social interaction?" Then we let the participants experience a process of forming norms and values based on a shared experience.

Reading through the processes above, one can see that the different integrated elements of the seminar illustrate different paradigms of the three main traditional scientific disciplines. The seminar first leads the participants into a natural science inspired psychological mapping, gathers the outcomes of that mapping into a social process, described by social sciences, where participants in same colour groups jointly create the language categories of Red, Blue and Green, before the seminar process takes a humanistic turn by bringing the whole group back together to reflect on the process of identifying and constructing the categories.

Summary and learning points

This chapter presents a second type of deep level diversity that has been created through education and professional practice. There are similar underlying factors when people communicate and experience perceived differences. The differences are all relevant to the identity of the individual, they are embedded in *language, intertwined with different values, emotions are involved* and important elements of these diversities are *unconscious*.

In the professional arena, some people have such a dedication to their professional education that it can make it difficult to see and acknowledge other professions' valuable contributions. Paradigms are the shared basic assumptions and practices that underlie distinct scientific disciplines and can differ greatly between those disciplines. Some departments in organisations evolve a departmental culture that reflects the way members see and approach shared challenges and tasks. These distinct departmental cultures are named epistemic cultures. Conflicting epistemic cultures might also develop as a result of nearness to the customer versus hierarchy or professional staff units with separated functions.

In the Diversity Icebreaker seminar the language categories of Red, Blue and Green are created together through self-identification and forming of colour specific groups. The function of categorisation for cultural development can then be revealed through collective reflection on the overall Diversity Icebreaker seminar process.

Bibliography

Alvesson, M. (1996). *Communication, Power, and Organisation*. Berlin/New York: de Greyter

Arvonen, J. & Ekvall, G. (1996). Effective leadership style both universal and contingent? Reports from the Department of Psychology No. 819. Stockholm, Sweden: University of Stockholm, Department of Psychology

Ekelund, B.Z. & Maznevski, M.L. (2008). Diversity training: Are we on the right track? In B.Z. Ekelund & E. Langvik, *Diversity Icebreaker: How to Manage Diversity Processes* (pp. 131–148). Oslo: Human Factors Publishing

Habermas, J. (1981). *Theorie des Kommunikativen Handels. Band I und II*. Frankfurt am Main: Suhrkamp

Hiebert, P.G. (2008). *Transforming Worldviews: An Anthropological Understanding of How People Change*. Grand Rapids, MI: Baker Academic

Hofstede, G. (1998). Identifying organizational subcultures: An empirical approach. *Journal of Management Studies*, 35(1): 12

Johnsen, E. (1978). Ledelseslære – baseret på dansk erfaringsmateriale. *Erhvervsøkonomisk Tidsskrift*, 42(1): 196–301

Jones, E.E. & Nisbett, R.E. (1972). The actors and observer: Divergent perspectives of the causes of behavior. *Journal of Personality and Social Psychology*, 27(2): 79–94.

Knorr Cetina, K. (1999). *Epistemic Cultures*. Cambridge MA: Harvard University Press

Kuhn, T.S. (1970). *The Structure of Scientific Revolutions*. Chicago: University of Chicago Press

Margerison, C. & McCann, D. (1991). *Team Management. Practical Approaches*. London: Mercury Books

Maznevski, Martha L. (1994). Understanding our differences: Performance in decision-making groups with diverse members. *Human Relations*, 47(5): 531–535

Scharmer, C.O. & Kaufer, K. (2013). *Leading from the Emerging Future. From Ego-system to Eco-System Economics*. San Francisco: Berret-Koehler

Schein, E.H. (1985). *Organizational Culture and Leadership*. San Francisco: Jossey-Bass

Stenberg, R. (1999). *Organisationslogik i samverkan. Konsten att organisera samverkan i en imaginär organisation av offentlige aktörer*. Stockholm: Psykologiska Instituionen, Stockholms Universitet

Sørhaug, T. (1996). *Makt og tillit i moderne organisering*. Oslo: Universitetsforlaget

West, M.A., Borrill, C., Dawson, J., Scully, J., Carter, M., Anelay, S., Patterson, M. & Waring, J. (2002). The link between the management of employees and patient mortality in acute hospitals. *The International Journal of Human Resource Management*, 13 (8): 1299–1310

Whorf, B. (1956). *Language, Thought & Reality*. Cambridge, MA: MIT Press

6 Ethno-geographical cultural differences

Early in my career I was asked to give a conflict management course for Sami families/first nation people in North Norway. One of their challenges was that the herds of reindeer had increased to a volume that challenged the capability of the land to reproduce enough grass and moss. I was standing there at the city hall's main meeting room, 9 o'clock in the morning, precise and prepared. There was no one there. I was frustrated. I felt ignored. All my preparatory work seemed to be of no use. After ten minutes a man looked into the room, saw me, and asked "Are you the white man?" I understood he applied metaphors that I normally associated with cowboy cartoons that I had read during my upbringing. "Yes, I am." I answered. He replied "Then, you do not know, I see, that we do not start on time here." My associations from what I had read about other cultures popped up in my mind, together with some ideas about coping when you are in a foreign country. I asked "And, what do we do, in order to get started?" He answered "If you and I walk around in the centre of the city, people will understand that you have come, and then they will come here to attend the seminar." And, so we did, and it worked out well. The only person that was frustrated, felt ignored and not respected, was myself.

Cross-cultural meetings

This was a typical example of a frustrating moment of learning. It illustrates the surprises in cross-cultural meetings and the emotional frustration that pops up before one is able to think twice. When I started to tell the story as an illustration of cross-cultural differences, I could see the funny parts. And it happened inside my own country, but with the minority culture of first nation people up north in my country. For me, it was a reminder of what I call the "moments of surprise" – the meeting with the Others and the surprise is there because of lack of awareness or knowledge about the Other's culture. This "moment of surprise" can be tipped into a negative experience or a positive learning process. The importance of avoiding either a fight and flight response has been mentioned earlier. In the field of cross-cultural mastery, the concept of "sustained judgement" has been pointed out as being central in navigating these "moments of surprise". The concept underlines the importance of recognising your first emotional reaction and leaving aside cognitive judgement of the Other in a negative way. The next step: Start rethinking, analyse the situation for alternative ways of seeing and do not forget to ask the Other to explain what is going on from their point of view. And, then we are back again to the communicative elements described in Chapter 3.

Definition of culture

Culture is one of the concepts that has been defined in many ways over the last 50 years. In the area of cross-cultural psychology and management, in his seminal book in 1980 Geert Hofstede defines culture as a "software of the mind" and "shared mental models that condition individuals' responses to environment". This definition stresses the perceptions and actions that people have in common when they belong to the same cultural group.

Another way of approaching the concept of culture is to define what are the necessary characteristics needed in order to use the cultural concept (Lane et al., 2004; Thomas & Inkson, 2003). The following list enlarges the perspective of culture, and defines the concept in different contexts.

Culture is something that

- is shared with others
- is transferred through learning across generations
- influences the way we see and act
- is systematic and organised
- can be used to identify a group as different from other groups
- has some elements of unconsciousness
- is integrated in language

Edgar Schein (1985) applies the iceberg metaphor to describe levels of unconsciousness. What is on the top and what you see is what you consciously can see like in cultural artifacts, rituals and behaviours. Under the water level lie the subconscious elements of norms, attitudes and beliefs. People can become aware of these subconscious elements through reflection and communication. At the lowest level of the iceberg we find the unconscious level of basic assumptions and values. This level is tightly interwoven with language, or the "software of the mind" as Geert Hofstede called it. These are the structures which are difficult to grasp unless you reflect more deeply and discuss with Others catalysed by multiple "surprise moments".

This is a more advanced form of reflective learning, that is more easy accessible when you see things through the eyes of the Other. This advanced capability is what we aim for in this book and in the advanced used of the Diversity Icebreaker concept. You can read about cultural values, but your own values coming from your particular cultural heritage, belong to you as an individual, integrated into your behaviour and emotions, and accessible only through personal learning.

Culture and language

A very central part of culture is the language that we learn from our parents through our upbringing. It constitutes a framework for creating meaning in what we see. As shared in Chapter 3, the meaning created is also formed by the way we use language in our actions and communicative interaction (Wittgenstein, 1953). Language as such is created in the interaction between people as a tool for coordination and exchange of information and meaning. Language is different in different cultures, based upon cultural specific challenges. For example, the eskimos have many different words for describing different types of snow compared to other cultures. In Hindi, there are many words for different states of mind and consciousness, In Columbia, there are many words for corruption. One of my colleagues grew up bi-culturally in Japan with Japanese as the language she learned in the community and American English as the language at home. She said that it was difficult for her to be dominant and aggressive in the Japanese language. If she felt it important to express these qualities, she shifted to American English. The young "Nachwuchsgruppe" in Daimler Benz learnt it was more successful to ask one strict Director for favours in English than her native Hochdeutsch.

Given our perceptual limitations and structures, language is forming how we see what we see. The different words, concepts and metaphors also have different emotional connotations. For me, talking about myself as psychologist elicits good emotions. Talking about being Norwegian also bring good feelings when I work in peace-related activities in the Middle East. But, being Norwegian in a context of climate crisis and oil-production is a bit more problematic. We all have groups that we belong to, and identify with. I am man with a Norwegian cultural background. Categories are fixed and whether I can feel good or bad about these categories differs in different contexts. Others' view of me and the groups where I feel I belong also contribute to a positive and negative experience based on my identity. Norwegians are proud of their country. Being Norwegian in Norway is positive. But, what about being not-Norwegian in Norway? A logical consequence is that "this is not so positive". It illustrates that if you have a positive view of yourself, and you are setting the norms, it is most likely that the Others in this comparison will be evaluated less optimally. This is what Edward Said states clearly in his introduction to western perspectives on the oriental part of the world (Said, 1979).[1]

Some words have connotations of power and suppression. In the USA the word "black" has long been used in a negative and disparaging way. But, then the Afro-Americans themselves started to use it as an empowering and positive self-descriptive word. It turned into a symbol of taking power. And, at the same time, still, it was unacceptable for the white majority to use the word. It became a word that excluded and differentiated in a new way. The word had different functions based on who was using it. This illustrates that words become meaningful in different ways with different actors.

We often see that minority groups introduce and fight for new words that do not have a negative history in order to seek dignity and positivity by the naming. For people in the majority group who sympathise with these groups, it becomes a symbol for "being on the right side". Immigrants seem to be a group that quite often are renamed here in Norway. Ideas of political correctness and negative sanctions for those who do not follow the new ideals is a challenge for many who do not take part in these renaming processes. A central idea behind these initiatives is that words have an influence. But, if the words change and the world out there does not change, the new words will gradually represent the same reality. Repeated renaming illustrates the limitations of what change of wording can do by itself. Even so, the renaming process creates hope and symbolises ideas of a better future as well as sometimes allowing dialogue about subjects that were previously too loaded to broach. This creates energy and for this reason, can contribute to political power through collective action.

Self-insights in cross-cultural meetings

"I need Others to see my own blind zones" is one of the sentences I often use in order to make people appreciate Others' perspectives. The blind zones consist of elements that I am not aware of, like the basic assumptions and values as mentioned by Edgar Schein. Blind zones may also contain elements that are suppressed by myself as a consequence of my own defence mechanisms. Since they are suppressed, they influence my behaviour with Others without my awareness. For example, if I am afraid of meeting people from a very different culture, and I am ashamed of this fear, I might suppress it and start blaming Others when their own similar fears come up.[2] Both these sources of blind zones are potential learning points when participants in seminars give each other feedback.

When people from different cultures meet, the blind zone has other elements. When people from different cultures meet, when Others meet Others, their awareness about their own qualities emerges out of which of their own qualities are experienced as different in comparison with the Others. As mentioned in an earlier chapter referring to works of Saussure and Bateson, it is the perceived relative difference that makes each Other aware of one's own unique quality (Culler 1976; Bateson, 1972). This implies that the Other is just as important, if not more important, as oneself in the understanding of one's own cultural identity. Let me take an example: When I, as a Norwegian, meet "typical Germans" in business meetings, I realise that I am a bit sloppy about being on time. If I meet Spanish people, I might think that I am the one showing respect for time while the Spanish are not. My understanding of my cultural values is a consequence of who I meet. As such, my self-understanding is formed by my social interaction with Others.

Can I see myself from the perspective of the Other? Only through asking the Other to share their view of me and often it is hard for the other to be explicit. Can even this lead to a true representation of myself through the Other's eyes? No, because I have to perceive and evaluate the Other's story through my own worldview. And then, my understanding of the Other's background, motive, the meaning of the context I am in and more – is my own contribution to the way I understand the Other's story about perceiving me. In practice, we have to use words and understand sentences in a communication game where we practice communication, interacting and acting together – and where the whole interaction between these phenomena is jointly constructing the meaning of myself, the Other and the context through words.[3] When it seems that we can talk and act together in harmony, we seem to have found a way of understanding that gives us the feeling of shared understanding. This feeling is there when you do not experience broken expectations, you do not experience emotional reactions you do not understand or conflicting values that you cannot foresee etc.

We often use a *perceptual filter* as a metaphor for how our own cultural background limits our own perspective of the Other. The filter forms what you see, and what comes to your attention. If you have a traditional European background and you meet an Islamic woman wearing a hijab, your awareness of her costume is much more heightened since you are not used to this. She is wearing different clothes from what you are used to. So, this is what you see – and you might ignore many other sides of the interaction due to this interesting distraction. At the same time – you might have a filter called "women's lib".

Seen from your cultural background, you may see the hijab and any mandatory use of the hijab as a contrast to your own cultural norms, and this triggers an emotional reaction and point of view. If your filter is called "women lib, European" –when you see the Other – the Other wearing a hijab will create a reaction in you that is defined by you. The filter metaphor illustrates that what you see is a reduction, and at the same time what you see is also your own filter. It can easily be illustrated if you imagine a vertical filter that only lets light come through your senses in vertical lines. You can see the object out there and create an image of it – but what you see is a snapshot of the object organised in vertical lines, not the whole object.

So it follows that people from different cultures will see and perceive the same phenomena differently, but they do not see this difference before they are able to take the perspective of the Other. Their perceptual filter created by their own culture stands as a contrasting difference to the perceptual filters of people from other cultures. In order to see both your own filter as well as the Other's filter, you have to ask questions in a way that the Other can describe how they perceive the situation as well as how they perceive you. This interactive exchange of information and creation of meaning is the process whereby each person can learn more about the Other and oneself at the same time.

You might change your attitude about yourself by being aware, not of a blind zone of an internal quality, but of a quality of difference that was made clear through interacting with an Other. The interaction per se makes it possible to see these two perspectives. Additionally, seeing more perspectives that include perspectives that are rooted in persons from other cultures, makes you more knowledgeable about cultural differences with yourself as an actor. Knowledge is an important component in the competence of interacting cross-culturally. A change in the ideas of the cultural background of the Other leads to a new understanding of the Other in your next meeting. Your new presumptions are different from your old presumptions.

We have through this cross-cultural meeting illustrated how meaning is created and how self-understanding evolves through interaction between two actors. If we do not take the perspective from an actor's point of view, but as an observer of two or more actors, including ourselves, we can see patterns of interaction that can be identified in different ways. The observer position, which is the position that I described earlier in Chapter 4 (when I presented the reflecting team and trialogue), gives an opportunity to study the interaction at another level. You might call it a higher logical level, because you can study interactions from an outside perspective in multiple situations with many people. This type of knowledge is what typically is created in social sciences based upon large data, comparisons and patterns of similarities and differences across large numbers of unique observations.[4]

For example, in the interaction I was describing above where Germans were prepared in time, and the Norwegians are a bit more sloppy, and Spanish people did not think this had much importance, I can ask myself "What is the underlying common quality that this is about?" and, the answer could be "Time". There might be a quality or approach to time that varies across cultures. In some cultures, it is important to organise taking time as an important central consideration and then a shared cultural expectation to respect time schedules is a consequence. If time is not that important – or if other aspects are more important, such as interpersonal interaction, then the behaviour shown will be different from that of the Germans. This is where cross-cultural psychology adds value with a particular type of knowledge. I will now introduce what in this research field are often called "cultural dimensions".

Cultural dimensions as useful concepts

Both in social anthropology as well as cross-cultural psychology, concepts are introduced with the aim of reducing the complexity of describing different cultures. In social anthropology, researchers have normally approached other cultures by observation of Others, and sometimes participative observation. Researchers have tried to see the other culture from within, from the Others' perspective, even though the very fact of their presence as an outsider can change the Others' behaviour. General differences have been formulated by different researchers.

An example is E. Hall (1966) who noted the differences between low-context and high-context cultures. In high context cultures, you need to see the context in order to understand the meaning of the utterances. In low-context cultures, the meaning is more easily understood from the utterances themselves. In cross-cultural psychology, the similarities and differences between cultures has been the major approach very often using questionnaires based on western logic and large samples with analysis of large amounts of data. This quantitative logical approach with the outsider as the actor, has been named *Etic, in contrast to Emic*. Emic is about seeing it from within, through the eyes of the Other. Emic generates descriptions that are broad and thick with many variable nuances and uniqueness. In contrast, etic is about creating general and robust knowledge that can be applied in many contexts.

Cultural dimensions have typically emerged out of different types of statistical analysis like factor analysis and cluster analysis. The data most often comes from individuals filling in questionnaires. The conceptual ideas of dimensions emerge out of analysis of the large data. Cultures can then be described through positioning them at different levels of the different dimensions. When you approach people from other cultures these dimensions can be applied as conceptual categories that make you more aware of differences that might cause communication challenges. Just like personality dimensions, and just like Red, Blue and Green, the cultural dimensions can be concepts that can make you more competent in being aware, seeing and have a broader repertoire of behaviour in interaction with the Other (Bird et al., 2000).

Many of the dimensions that are tested as being relevant across cultures emerged from anthropology and social action theory (e.g. Mead, 1934; Parsons & Shils, 1951). Cultural differences show up as statistical differences across aggregated individual data, usually categorised by the different nation states that the individuals were born into. This can result in the temptation to apply normative generalisations to individuals. This outcome has resulted in a conflict ridden discourse and debate among major academics about the correctness and usefulness of mapping individuals this way, as well as defining and categorising any one individual based on their country of birth using questionnaires designed for large data cultural analysis (Hofstede, 2001). The core of the debate is that generalised categories emerge out of differences in large data and for this reason are not well fitted for an accurate description of any one individual.

A sensible personal resolution of this debate is to be aware of this limitation and to know that individual self-understanding has evolved for the individual through her or his history in interaction with Others and through reflecting on these experiences (Løvlie-Schibbye, 1983). Reading and learning about yourself through literature and psychological assessment is part of the repertoire of available learning processes for individuals as well as for collectives, communities and societies. Through these activities, science contributes to change for both the individual and the society (Skjervheim, 1959). Comparing and interrelating yourself to the general knowledge about a society is one way to understand and change yourself.

An example of this is how it has been possible for me to write this book in the way that I have done. The book is written with a clear voice of myself as an individual in a Norwegian context using English as a second language. My Norwegian context gives me some particular ideas about the uniqueness of Norwegian culture compared to other cultures. My personal identity has mainly been set by my upbringing, but the position I take as a proud Norwegian writing this book has only been made possible through my gaining more scientific and globally shared knowledge. Through this globalised knowledge I can guide myself in choosing how to present my work. This knowledge is central to the act of writing this book, as a Norwegian in a Norwegian context.

Which cultural dimensions are relevant?

Given the idea that categories of cultural dimensions might be helpful in meeting with Others, the question is which ones are most essential to increase one's own awareness and competence when interacting with Others? Which dimensions are most useful for building the basis for initiating a conversation to define and describe one's own culture and that of an Other?

In this field of cross-cultural psychology, the work of Geert Hofstede stands out. In short, he gathered data through an employee survey from 116,000 people in one globally dispersed US company (Hofstede, 1980). When he analysed the data, there were differences among the nationalities in the company that could not be explained by ordinary organisational concepts and explanations. Searching the literature of anthropology and social action, he evolved four dimensions that differentiated different national cultures. With the partnership of Michael Bond in Hong Kong and others he added two more later. His work and the application of his models in multinational organisations are so central to international management theory that it can be said he became seen as a Founding Father figure in this field; Work that many scholars either relate to or differentiate themselves from. His work enabled others to work with culture as a concrete variable, even though in itself it is a concept that remains indefinable and fuzzy.

So, the idea that the cross-cultural field has or will converge to some static conclusion is a naïve idea of how social sciences grow. Kuhn's comments about different schools of paradigmatic traditions can die when main figures and institutions leave the field.

If you ask which dimensions have been the most researched (see Kirkman, Lowe & Gibson, 2006), individualism versus collectivism (or degree of individualism) first defined by Margaret Mead (1934) and authority/power distance are most frequent.[5] There is one researcher Harry Triandis (1995) who has repeatedly stated a 2 x 2 model with these dimensions. I took part in a research project where we studied different ways of reacting to violations of psychological contract, and found that this model was very applicable, when describing meaningful differences between countries (Thomas et al., 2010).

Given my earlier caution that the interpretation and so the actual meaning of an utterance depends on the context and worldview of the Other, it is equally important to be aware that how these two seemingly robust "etic" dimensions actually manifest in different cultures will require "emic" analysis. Not to do this local and "emic" analysis will be what Hofstede defines as the "core ecological fallacy" (Hofstede, 1980). This point highlights that it is in fact impossible to define "culture" separately from the constructs we use to measure it by. The measurement of cultural dimensions garnered by aggregating individual questionnaires is static and there is no theory connecting these generalised static value dimensions to the interaction and adaptive learning behaviours we are exploring in this book. Nevertheless, when these dimensions are understood only as pegs from which to start a journey and conversation into a dynamic evolving landscape, and not as ends in themselves, they can be very useful.

So, these two dimensions, Individual versus collectivism and one's relationship to authority, can be seen as essential and there are others that are also helpful in many cross-cultural interactions. In a project start-up book I highlighted nine cross-cultural dimensions that I found relevant when consulting with international projects (Esnault & Ekelund, 2008). I shall use these dimensions as a good recommendation for what can be helpful to think about when engaging in the eye-opening process of meeting Others.

1   Power distance: the degree to which power is shared unequally with large or small distance to the people in power (emerging out of inequality studies and coalesced in Hofstede (1980)).

2   Individualism versus collectivism: the degree to which a person or context focuses on the individual or the group (Mead 1934 and almost all models after that).

3   Focusing first on the task – task oriented – versus focusing on knowing the person – people oriented – and allowing the task to emerge (close to specificity versus diffuseness (Parson & Shils, 1951)).

4   Uncertainty avoidance: the degree to which people build and follow beliefs, structures, processes, and rules to avoid uncertainty about the future (Hofstede, 1980).

5   Time: long time versus short time perspective (Hofstede & Bond, 1988) Past, Present, Future (Kluckhohn & Strodtbeck, 1961), Circular versus linear time (Hall, 1959).

6   Universalism versus particularism: general rules versus every situation and relationship decides what is the best decision (Parsons & Shils 1951; Trompenaars, 1993).

7   High-context versus low-context: high context implies that things have to be seen in context so that we can understand them (Hall, 1966).

8   Neutral or emotional: formal and task oriented and emotionally restrained versus open and emotionally engaged (Parson & Shils, 1951; Trompenaars, 1993; Lewis, 1996).

9   Monochronic versus polychronic: doing one thing at a time, or doing lots of things at the same time (Hall, 1959).

These dimensions can be functional starting points and eye-openers as well as filters. They may help you become aware of cultural values and assumptions that are lying behind another person's reaction, a reaction that may cause emotional frustration, representing a "moment of surprise" in your interaction with the Others. These dimensional filters can also function as helping guidelines in the sense-making process (Bird et al., 2000).

Cultural distance

Based on the different empirical traditions, it is possible to identify and rank/order countries based on how aggregated data from individuals from that country score on the different dimensions.[6] This can help to roughly indicate the potential cultural difference between your own culture and the culture to which the Other belongs. As a rule of thumb, it is more likely that differences, surprises and challenges will occur where people from quite distant cultures meet. I come from Norway, and we do not respect authority very much. And we are more people-oriented than task-oriented. Many other societies are much more obedient to authority compared to us. So, when our leaders move to another country where the leader is expected to take charge and give directions and commands, the Norwegian leader often fails to fulfil such expectations given the Norwegian supportive and facilitative leadership style. In contrast, when leaders come from many other countries in the world, they have a huge challenge learning and adapting to the socially interactive inclusive communication that is needed to establish legitimacy as a leader in Norway. I normally say that if a foreign top manager makes a decision on his own at the top, and sends a written message to the employees about the decision, the employees will file the letter as a curiosity in their drawer in case people would like to see that form of communication. They will not care about the content.

Even though a large cultural distance is something that increases the likelihood of surprises, the concept of *cross-cultural paradox* is based on the surprising experiences shared between people that *think* they belong to the same culture and for this reason expect sameness and shared expectations. When they register surprise that meetings do not evolve as expected, they can get extraordinarily indignant and frustrated, and even dismissive and derogatory, compared to when they approach an Other where they expect differences to be a part of the game (O'Grady & Lane, 1996). It seems that the disappointment of reality not living up to expectations has elements of feeling deceived and betrayed, emotions that kick off stronger reactions. Swedish culture is more task oriented than Norwegian culture. But, we all think that we belong to the same Scandinavian culture. So, when we work together with Swedes, we collide. Swedes stay more focused on business whereas Norwegians prefer small talk to get to know each other. Both sides get surprised and frustrated.

In 1999, I was in Bosnia with colleagues and trained participants in organisations involved in building democratic institutions after the war in the 1990s when Yugoslavia fell apart.[7] There was a mix of people coming from the three religious cultural groups in Bosnia and from other western European democracies. Together with the cross-cultural expert Martha Maznevski, I made assumptions about cultural differences based upon general country differences in line with existing empirical data at country level. Then we let each person answer a questionnaire on cultural values and compared with our hypotheses. Nine out of 11 hypotheses were not confirmed. Instead of refuting the empirical models that were our starting point, it made us reflect on the

characteristics of the samples we analysed. We realised that the Bosnian participants were not typical representatives nor in a typical employer situation.
They were well educated, relatively young and ambitious in promoting their
career in a western European cooperative organisation.

The western European participants were a group of people that socio-
logically belonged to the international recruited "helpers and developers".
What we learned from this is that when such collaborations are set up, those
recruited are not typically representative, with values aligned with what is most
normal in the country from which they come. They did not represent the
statistical mean in the country data gathered (Maznevski & Ekelund, 2004).
Often this is not the case in such collaborative initiatives and processes. Equally,
an economic migrant that individually decides to move to another country far
away is probably a more courageous, competent, adventure seeker and self-
confident than may be typical in their source country. When large groups of
refugees collectively escape an area, we might expect a broader and more
representative group in relation to cultural values. Having come through a
painful and traumatising experience, recent migrants often struggle to acclima-
tise to a new host country. They are unlikely to immediately be at their best or
be able to represent themselves as they would in their previous cultures.

Cross-cultural experience as a surprising enlightening experience

For each of us it is important to be aware of the type of knowledge being
created from large data analysis with country differences. The above illustration
from Bosnia is an illustration where Martha Maznevski and I wanted to show
that assessment of the individual in the specific context was a more important
platform for self-understanding and interaction than generic knowledge about
country differences. So, let us assume that a person meets an Other from
another culture, the country differences on cultural dimensions is the knowledge of the Other's culture that mainly influence his/her presumptions. Then,
when the "moment of surprise" suddenly erupts, the accessible mental models
are misleading. For this reason, to be able to manage this interaction well needs
more specific and precise information about the person, context and background. Asking questions and exploring the Other's background and worldview is probably more relevant than the ideas positioning the individual
somewhere on a limited dimensional scale based upon country of origin.

This "moment of surprise" can often end in fight or flight responses, as mentioned earlier. My ambition with this book is to make this "moment of surprise"
into an experiential opportunity for each person to learn more about themself, the
Other individual, the Other group, as well as how to master the interaction in a
culturally intelligent way. I use the phrase culturally intelligent because it was a
term that was introduced in 2003/3 (Early & Ang, 2003; Thomas & Inkson, 2003)
with a more precise focus on the learning processes in an intercultural meeting.

In my writing so far, I have focused on the challenge of meeting Others,
with fight and flight as natural responses due to uncertainty, anxiety and

sometimes fear. As stated, this book's ambition is to increase the feeling of mastery and develop the ability to meet Others in a positive way. There is one area of cross-cultural meetings where positive experiences have been the main driver, and that is the international tourist industry. Tourists themselves decide to spend lots of money in order to experience another culture. We assume that they do this because they expect to have positive experiences meeting different people within another culture. In 2010 I took part in a research, development and training program in international tourism (Samuelsen et al., 2010). We applied the Cultural Intelligence model (Thomas et al., 2008) and started to study the interaction between tourist guides and tourists. We wanted to see if we could learn about how a cross-cultural meeting with "moments of surprise" could become a surprisingly positive experience.

The value proposition here was to design a context and interactive meeting where the psychological experience was so great that the tourists would share the experience positively with others in their home country. We were inspired by the Flow concept of Mihaly Csikszentmihaly (1990) where the level of tension should be high, but not too high. We thought that the major value created by the tourist would be a learning experience where the tourist's own history and identity were involved, and also that this learning experience should be designed inside a context of interacting with elements or stories from the local culture of the tourist destination. The tourist guides were trained to acknowledge the tourists' attendance, curiosity and learning through interaction. For this reason, we let the tourists' self-managed activity be the one that decided the level of challenge. Instead of having a focus on the story told locally about the local history, we created an experiential value where the customers' story of surprises, learning and growth was central. Moments of surprise, experiences beyond expectations and peak experiences became the focus for their stories told back home as a confirmation of their successful travel.

Connecting ideas

I started this chapter with my surprising moment in the Sami society. I was able to transform this story into a positive learning experience. The Bosnian experience was also a challenging experience with positive learning, but by then I had more competence. It was also the first time I applied the Diversity Icebreaker in a politically and culturally challenging situation. I have continued this learning process by integrating my competence of trust when I started to work with peace-related activities in the Middle East, which will be presented more thoroughly in Chapter 9. As mentioned at the beginning of this book, I see the need for such a competence when people start to move across countries and continents. In order to solve ecological crises we also have to find solutions together across national boundaries. Intercultural competence is, for this reason, an absolute necessity in order to solve these huge challenges.

Summary and learning points

1   In our cultural upbringing, we learn the basics of language and relating to each Other, an upbringing that is rooted in an ethnic group in a geographical area. This is the societal cultural heritage.
2   Cultural identity and values are formed by this upbringing; it becomes accessible to conscious awareness in a cross-cultural meeting.
3   Cultural dimensions are concepts that help us to make sense across different kinds of cultural settings. These dimensions, though, emerge out of analyses of large data and have limited usefulness when individuals meet.
4   But, cultural dimensions might be helpful guidelines in the first part of the sense making of meeting Others. Then more advanced understanding and personal precise knowledge will evolve through the learning experience of interacting with the individual person.
5   Cross-cultural meetings do not need to end in fight-or-flight responses, but can be enjoyable self-reflective learning moments.

Notes

1 I was invited in 2013 in Beirut to take part in the ceremony for "Arabic women of the year". It was repeatedly stated from the different winners that they did not want the European women's lib norms concerning freedom and power in their own countries. They saw different opportunities and strategies for influence than what was preached by western representatives. They wanted to find their way of modernity, different from the western form.
2 Projective identification is the process of projecting uncomfortable elements in yourself onto others, and then relating to it as a perceived quality of the other person. Sometimes you project uncomfortable elements that you repress internally (Klein, 1947). Then you can act towards this externalised quality, for example with disgust or negativity. Sometimes you project what you have as dreams and ideals, and this leads to a positive identification and need of being close to the other, in order to internalise positive elements of yourself (Løvlie-Schibbye, 1983).
3 This perspective of creation of meaning is aligned with Wittgenstein´s late contributions to the understanding of language in the *Philosophic Foundations* (Wittgenstein, 1953).
4 The metaphor of "higher lever" is a metaphor that certainly contributes to a positive self-image of academics doing this type of research. But is it a higher level? No, it is just a different type of knowledge, a knowledge that through larger empirical work, conceptual models based upon larger data, theories and production of articles create an industry of knowledge workers named scholars and academics. This is just another language game. A game on enlightenment that both is good for science as well as helpful in practice.
5 I analysed through a factor analysis the country scores from four different empirical traditions that have published data on country differences, which also confirms that these two dimensions are common across all four traditions of cultural dimensions. The main traditions were Hofstede's large studies (Hofstede, 2001), globe studies of values (House, 2004), Smith & Peterson's critical incidents (Smith et al., 2003), personal communication) and Maznevski´s cultural perspectives based upon Kluckhohn & Strodtbeck's concepts (Maznevski, personal communication).

6 For example: https://www.hofstede-insights.com/product/compare-countries
7 This was the first time Diversity Icebreaker was applied in a multi-cultural context. Following my peace promoting activities in the Middle East I presented a paper telling the story from Norway, through Balkan to the Middle East (Ekelund, 2013).

Bibliography

Alvesson, M. (1996). *Communication, Power, and Organisation*. Berlin/New York: de Gruyter

Bateson, G. (1972). *Steps to an Ecology of Mind*. New York: Ballantine Books

Bird, A., Osland, J., Delano, J. & Jacob, M. (2000). Beyond sophisticated stereotyping: Cultural sensemaking in context. *Academy of Management Executive*, 14(1): 65–79

Csikszentmihalyi, M. (1990), *Flow: The Psychology of Optimal Experience*. New York: Harper and Row

Culler, J. (1976). *Saussure*. Glasgow: Fontana/Collins

Earley, P.C. & Ang, S. (2003). *Cultural Intelligence: Individual Interactions across Cultures*. Stanford: Stanford University Press

Ekelund, B.Z. (2013). Diversity Icebreaker applied in conflict management from Norway, through the Balkans to the Middle East. SIETAR Europe conference in Tallinn, 20 Sept 2013. Presented in B.Z. Ekelund & P. Pluta (Eds.) (2015). *Diversity Icebreaker II. Further Perspectives*. Oslo: Human Factors Publishing

Esnault, M. & Ekelund, B.Z. (2008). *Project Start-up. No Time to Hurry*. Oslo: Human Factors

Hall, E.T. (1959). *The Silent Language*. Greenwich, CT: Fawcett

Hall, E.T. (1966). *The Hidden Dimension*. Garden City, NY: Doubleday

Hofstede, G. (1980). *Culture's Consequences: International Differences in Work-related Values*. Beverly Hills: Sage

Hofstede, G. & Bond, M.H. (1988). The Confucius connection: From cultural roots to economic growth. *Organizational Dynamics*, 16(4): 4–21

Hofstede, G. (2001). *Culture's Consequences*. Second edition. Thousand Oaks: Sage

House, R.J., Hanges, P.J., Javidan, M., Dorfman, P.W. & Gupta, V. (2004). *Culture, Leadership, and Organizations: The GLOBE Study of 62 Societies*. Thousand Oaks, CA: Sage

Klein, M. (1947). Analysis of a schizophrenic state with depersonalization. *International Journal of Psychoanalysis*, 28: 130–139

Kirkman, B.L., Lowe, K.B. & Gibson, C.B. (2006). A quarter century of *Culture's Consequences*: A review of empirical research incorporating Hofstede's cultural values framework. *Journal of International Business*, 37: 285–320

Kluckhohn, F. & Strodtbeck, F. (1961). *Variations in Value Orientations*. Evanston, IL: Row, Peterson

Lane, H.W., Mendenhall, M., Maznevski, M.L. & McNett, J. (2004). *Handbook of Global Management. A guide to Managing Complexity*. MA: Blackwell Publishing

Løvlie-Schibbye, A.L. (1983). *The Self*. Oslo: Universitetsforlaget

Lewis, R. (1996). *When Cultures Collide. Leading across Cultures*. Boston: Nicholas Brealy International

Margerison, C. & McCann, D. (1991). *Team Management. Practical Approaches*. London: Mercury Books

Maznevski, M.L. (1994). Understanding our differences: Performance in decision-making groups with diverse members. *Human Relations*, 47(5): 531–535

Maznevski, M.L. & Ekelund, B.Z. (2004). Cultural dimensions in action: Democratic elections in post-war Bosnia. *Organisational Theory and Practice; Scandinavian Journal of Organisational Psychology*, 1

Mead, M. (1934). *Mind, Self and Society*. Chicago: University Press

O'Grady, S. & Lane, H.W. (1996). The psychic distance paradox. *Journal of International Business Studies*, June, 27(2): 309–333

Parsons, T. & Shils, E. (1951). *Toward a General Theory of Action*. Cambridge, MA: Harvard University Press

Said, E.W. (1979). *Orientalism*. New York: Vintage Books

Samuelsen, R., Løvland, J., Søfting, E. & Ekelund, B.Z. (2010). Experience based value creation, an explorative tool development and organisational learning. (Norwegian text) NF Report 1001/2010

Scharmer, C.O. & Kaufer, K. (2013). *Leading from the Emerging Future. From Ego-System to Eco-System Economics*. San Francisco: Berret-Koehler

Schein, E.H. (1985). *Organizational Culture and Leadership*. San Francisco: Jossey-Bass

Skjervheim, H. (1959). *Objectivism and the Study of Man*. Mag. Degree Univ. of Oslo.

Sørhaug, T. (1996). *Makt og tillit i moderne organisering*. Oslo: Universitetsforlaget

Smith, P.B., Andersen, J.A., Ekelund, B.Z., Graversen, G. & Ropo, A. (2003). In search of Nordic management styles. *Scandinavian Journal of Management*, 19: 491–507

Thomas, D.C. & Inkson, K. (2003). *Cultural Intelligence: People Skills for Global Business*. San Francisco, CA: Berret-Koehler

Thomas, D.C., Ekelund, B.Z. et al. (2008). Cultural intelligence: Domain and assessment. *International Journal of Cross Cultural Management*, 8(2): 123–143

Thomas, D.C., Ekelund, B.Z. et al. (2012). Development of the Cultural Intelligence Assessment. *Advances of Global Leadership*, 7

Thomas, D.C., Fitzsimmons, S.R., Ravlin, E.C., Au, K., Ekelund, B.Z. & Barzantny, C. (2010). Psychological contracts across cultures. Perceptions and responses to violations. *Organization Studies*, 31: 1437–1458

Triandis, H.C. (1995). *Individualism and Collectivism*. Boulder, CO: Westview Press

Trompenaars, F. (1993). *Riding the Waves of Culture: Understanding Cultural Diversity in Business*. Avon: The Bath Press

Whorf, B. (1956). *Language, Thought & Reality*. Cambridge, MA: MIT Press

Wittgenstein, L. (1953). *Philosophical Investigations*. London: Wiley-Blackwell

Introduction to Chapters 7, 8 and 9

"Mam, there is man from Norway who wants to talk with you on the phone!" "Stop kidding."

In 1997 I read in an article that there were some research groups that mapped cultural values at individual level that could be used for giving feedback to the individual. I called one of the persons named in the most recent references, Martha Maznevski. The above quote was what I heard when her daughter answered the phone one Saturday morning in the USA. She sent me her PhD from 1994 in which she had documented that giving communication training to multicultural teams increased the quality of the team's problem solving. Mapping cultural values was part of the developmental work. It was built on the theoretical positions of Kluckhohn & Strodtbeck (1961) that had earlier been applied in cross-cultural training for businesses. I invited her to Norway and this kicked off years of cooperation both in research and business. She built the communication training on the work of Rolf Mikkel Blakar (1981) from Norway that she found by surprise in the cellar of the library in London, Ontario, Canada, which also was central to my psychology education. When we exchanged experiences from our different work with diversity in team processes, we realised that we had worked on three different types of diversities, those based on differences in personality, differences in scientific and professional paradigms, and socio-cultural differences.

We both agreed that the "solution" to the challenges was good communication. In her model for communication training, called Mapping-Bridging-Integrating, she applied Blakar's model (Blakar, 1984), but she added the integration of multiple ideas into a collective solution at the last stage. This is where she expands the communication between two Others into multiple people creating a solution together based upon the different contributions from the team members. In that way, her training integrates people's ideas into a joint solution.

Good communication is something that can be described as a form with no content. The content I have taken into consideration in this book is the three main deep-level diversity categories – personality, paradigms and culture – built on three different traditions.

1. The first diversity, personality, embraces the personal development of the individual through familiar upbringing and the forming of personality through near relations. With the introduction of Red, Blue and Green, the focus of this book has been on personal preferences for how people treat information when they solve problems together.

2. The second diversity was about the scientific and professional paradigms that constitute the educational platforms for professions.
3. The third diversity is about the cultural values that everyone in each society is raised in and absorbs from previous generations.

They are all differences that have something in common in spite of major differences in their development. They are all important for identity, inter-twined with values, emotionally connected, partly unconscious and integrated into language (Ekelund & Maznevski, 2008). For this reason, the "moments of surprise" are a challenge to repeatedly master across all these three diversities.

In these next three chapters I will focus on three different outcomes: crea-tivity and innovation, efficiency, and inclusive community. At the end each chapter, I will present how the three diversities mentioned above are relevant for the topic of the chapter.

Chapter 7 will focus on creative processes in groups and then relate creativity to innovation. Chapter 8 will focus on efficiency, a concept that can be applied to innovative processes, but the main focus will be on the execution stage of implementation and action. Chapter 9 will focus on how building an inclusive community can be an important quality while simultaneously promoting crea-tivity, innovation and efficiency.

In these chapters, creativity and innovation emerge within the Green perspec-tive and processes, efficiency emerges within the Blue, while inclusive community emerges in the Red component of integrating people when perspectives and processes are the central elements of the work. The outcome, or the product, can be seen as Green creative and innovative outcomes, a Blue cost effective product or a Red inclusive community which is good for people. With these added shifts of focus, I apply the colours on the perspectives, processes and products extended beyond any individual personal qualities defined as preferences for how informa-tion is treated by the individual. From now on, we will include a conceptual understanding of Red, Blue and Green encompassing "people, perspectives, pro-cesses and products", which is in line with the overview presented in Chapter 2.

Bibliography

Blakar, R. M. (1984). Communication: *A Social Perspective on Clinical Issues.* Oslo: Universitetsforlaget.

Ekelund, B. Z. & Maznevski, M. L. (2008). Diversity Training: Are We on the Right Track? In Ekelund, B.Z. & Langvik, E. *Diversity Icebreaker: How to Manage Diversity Processes* (pp. 131–148). Oslo: Human Factors Publishing.

Kluckhohn, F. & Strodtbeck, F. (1961). *Variations in Value Orientations.* Evanston, IL: Row, Peterson.

Maznevski, Martha L. (1994). Understanding Our Differences: Performance in Deci-sion-Making Groups with Diverse Members. *Human Relations,* 47(5): 531–535.

7 Promoting Green creativity and innovation

The Diversity Icebreaker seminar is an experiential process where participants co-create the meaning of Red, Blue and Green. Afterwards they apply these categories in how they jointly define the problem. And, sometimes they apply these categories to organise the processes in order to solve the problem. This co-creation process among equals has inspired me to apply the model with groups of families that need help for housing due to lack of economic resources. Poverty is a serious problem and has serious implications for identity of individuals and families. Creativity is very often about bringing old ideas into new contexts and combining elements in a new way. I brought the Diversity Icebreaker process into the housing projects and since Diversity Icebreaker is about promoting change by exchange of perspectives between people, I needed to bring multiple families embedded in poverty into a shared group process. What we saw, as expected, was the reframing of self-identity in a positive way. Nevertheless, it surprised us to see how this group established a common ground due to lack of money, how they validated each Other and how this validation made them reformulate their view of bureaucrats in the social services. We saw that they co-created a feeling of worthiness and dignity and new perspectives of what were good solutions for themselves. We saw them taking opposing and critical positions towards each Other and formulating them inside the language of Red, Blue and Green. It seemed easier for them to voice alternative views through colourful roles, because it was less personal. The language of Red, Blue and Green seemed to establish the common ground of a co-created problem solving strategy, a different form of common ground that was characterised by poverty.

Creativity and innovation

Creativity is creating a new idea, or a product, that is different from what existed before; fresh and new for the user (Zaltman et al., 1973). Innovation is when new and different ideas are employed in a useful way and utilised efficiently (Dagestad, 2015). Innovation is, for this reason, more complex and needs to involve organisational resources in coordinated change management. Efficiency in the process of implementation and execution is of course an important criteria for success. For this reason, diversity in executive competence is more relevant to innovation compared to creativity where ideas and perspectives are more important. Innovation often requires more time, involves more people and improved structures to craft individual creative ideas into actual real world applications.

Nevertheless, creativity is the starting point for innovation. It is individuals who contribute and develop ideas. So the starting point is the individual. Most often people think that some people are more creative than others, which probably is true. But, there are also situations that can stimulate anyone to become more creative. Not criticising new ideas that are brought to the table is one of the norm setting rules in brainstorming that encourages individuals to contribute more ideas. Thus, the quality of the working climate that is created is something that can facilitate people's idea generation.

The next step is the interaction between people with different ideas, which leads to new solutions. The social interaction between individuals sharing ideas is a collective process of knowledge creation. It is important to actively manage the group processes and climate of interaction when individuals are working with ideas. I will first present a process model from a creative problem-solving process that I have found very helpful in setting a structure for creative processes. Afterwards, I will present in more detail the basic structures of how the interaction of ideas can lead to new ideas.

Very often I see people state that creativity will be increased by bringing people with diverse information and multiple perspectives into the same room, and new ideas will come out. Given the research that also tells us that bringing diverse people into the same team may be more costly than helpful (DiStefano & Maznevski, 2000), I think efficient quality outcomes are most likely if we are more precise about how people and ideas best connect in order to maximise the likelihood of adding value from diversity. This is the best practice sought in Chapter 1. For this reason, I shall present the basic structures of how ideas and activities can be combined and interplay to create a better result due to optimal interaction between ideas.

Innovative processes in groups

Van Gundy identifies three core dilemmas in creative problem solving in groups that are important to take into consideration (Van Gundy, 1981). The three main dilemmas are:

1   Individual versus group processes for creativity. The learning point here is to make sure that individuals prepare ideas before exchanging ideas. Let individuals do silent brainstorming. Let them make notes. When the social interaction starts, start with sharing the ideas that have been written.
2   Divergent versus convergent processes. Developing new ideas together is a process of opening up. It is called a divergent process. After opening up it is important to narrow down and focus on conclusions, which

represents a convergent process. The second process is very different from the first one, a stage shift where a shared understanding of moving to the next step is important. There are different ways of coming to a conclusion. Examples include through discussions, debates, voting, estimating the costs, exploring the impact and more, depending on the initial purpose and need.

3   Focusing on problem definition versus focusing on ideas for solving the problem. Most often people like to jump straight to the solution, as soon as a good enough solution comes to their mind. Spending more time to understand the problem before searching for solutions will most often lead to a better and more advanced understanding of the problem. This will usually lead to better suggestions for solutions.

This process can be illustrated in the following way. In Figure 7.1 the shades of grey represent colour dimensions illustrating different perspectives.

In this model all participants whether they have a Red, Blue or Green primary reference can contribute with Red, Blue and Green perspectives. It is not only predominantly Green people who need to contribute to idea generation. Indeed, there are some indications that people with Blue qualities are more creative as individuals when they get a strict structure; they can be more creative inside the box. There are also some indications that a rigid structure along the value chain of creative processes leads to innovative solutions that have a better chance of successful implementation (Boyd & Goldberg, 2013). We have from the beginning searched for different contexts that promote creative input from different types of people.

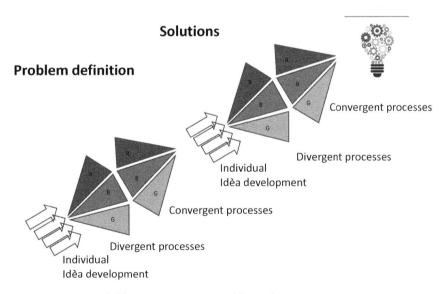

Figure 7.1 Steps and dilemmas in creative problem solving in groups

Three basic interactive forms for working innovative with ideas

As mentioned, a typical recommendation in the literature on creativity is to bring diverse people into the same room, and then assume and hope that new ideas will evolve. Figure 7.1 illustrates one way to make a step wise structure in these processes. The communication model Mapping-Bridging-Integrating overlaps this creative problem solving model. Mapping is the gathering of ideas, Bridging is the process and Integration is the merging of ideas at the end. But, still I find very few precise descriptions of how inter-action between ideas leads to something new. The Integration stage does not describe the integration beyond "building on and integrating each other's ideas" (DiStefano & Maznevski, 2000). In Van Gundy's recommendations there are different ways of creating agreements for debates and criteria for weighting solutions with pro and cons, but I have been puzzled by this lack of precision. Some 15 years ago, I wanted to do something better and started to categorise the different possibilities of idea-exchange. Seeing lots of ideas emerging through good dialogues made it possible for me to develop basic structures for how ideas can be building blocks in idea generation. My idea is that a good understanding of these major basic differences will make it pos-sible to understand, facilitate and manage creative idea generation better. One important part of this facilitation process is creating a shared under-standing among participants of "the rules of the game". Unless people have a shared understanding of the norms and forms, misunderstandings and distrust easily come up. This is a part of the Bridging process. Today I categorise these idea generation patterns in three different basic forms.[1]

1   The first form: How ideas and perspectives from an Other person influ-ence my own idea.
2   The second form: When many perspectives are in action in a coordinated systematic way.
3   The third form: When something pops up that is not logically connected.

The first form: How ideas and perspectives from an Other person influence my own idea

Reframing: The idea in light of the Other's ideas

The extent to which an idea is more or less meaningful depends on the con-text. Seeing the same idea from an Other's perspective implies a change in the context of the idea. The meaning is changed. If you see a good idea from another discipline, the value of the idea might turn out very different.

Example: A social worker can suggest an idea for the family, but they reject it because they do not trust the competence of the social worker. When the medical doctor, from the position of their higher prestige and authority, acknowledges the competence of the social worker, the family consider the idea with a different level of legitimacy.

Theory: Psychologists have used mirroring as a method to enhance the patient's insight. It seems that viewing things from the outside, or hearing what one is saying but voiced from a different perspective, leads to a different kind of understanding of the ideas. Different disciplines are systematically different in their use of methods, in deciding what is important to observe and which phenomena are valuable (Kuhn, 1962).

Interdisciplinary import (learning from others)

When people have had some experiences with other disciplines they might begin using models and ways of thinking from those disciplines.

Example: Aggression Replacement Therapy is a method used in kindergarten to train kids to control their aggressive behaviour. To apply the same model in stress-mastery among nurses is an adoption of a model in a new context. Another example is to use logistics from engineering in order to develop ideas for how to treat patients waiting for psychiatric treatment.

Theory: Many would argue that this form of importing ideas and models is the most common form of innovation; the diffusion of an existing idea into a new area. Very often the idea has to be re-contextualised (Brannen, 2004) in order to be adopted to new settings. In the case I presented in the beginning of this chapter, I applied the Diversity Icebreaker in groups of families in poverty. This application gave us new insights about co-creation processes and the potential empowerment of co-created understanding of self and situations, in turn triggering people's transformation.

Interdisciplinary control (one perspective dominates the other)

Different professions and people in certain positions are sometimes in conflict. This often happens in organisations where the professions are fighting over resources. Some professions have a tendency to control according to cost effectiveness, others from what is politically acceptable. Some professions possess more power than others and when this power is applied, a common reaction is a feeling of being overrun. New knowledge appears and develops when workers across power structures are forced to see their own contributions in the light of Others' understanding. Usually a person that is overruled this way becomes more aware of their own perspectives and values.

Example: Economists win over architects in a collaboration concerning the design of a new building. Doctors win over nurses in caring for patients with cancer. Leaders often have a holistic perspective, and the suggestions of individual professional groups can be belittled when a more holistic perspective is at play.

Theory: In organisations, higher level goals are often administered by persons higher up in the hierarchy. Professional hierarchies are often organisationally constructed with the "right" of particular professional disciplines to become engaged in higher authoritative roles. This often leads to a superior directing from the position of his/her profession while many subordinates cannot easily identify with it. Information flow, dialogue, involvement, and respect contribute to reducing frustration when decisions are made. But, as long as hierarchical structures and specialisation of work tasks exist, we cannot avoid the fact that those with responsibility for overall results will make decisions that run counter to the ideas of individual persons and professions lower in the hierarchy. Understanding this allows leaders to do something constructive.

The second form: When many perspectives are in action in a coordinated systematic way

Poly-disciplinary activities (administrative parallel split)

Tasks are divided and distributed among different professionals on the basis of who holds the expertise. The outcome is that individuals with different competences work side by side. This is a work form commonly used in bureaucracies and project work. New knowledge can develop through experience-based reflection where all involved evaluate their own and Others' contributions in relation to the end result.

Example: The mason lays bricks and the carpenter cuts roof planks and rafters.

Theory: This distribution of work tasks is a form that has probably existed forever. In the theoretical and historical context, it is Taylor's (1911) classical work on *The Principles of Scientific Management* that appears to be the earliest and clearest exposition of this kind of task distribution. Specialisation is after all, what causes teams and organisations to have greater efficiency. When the work tasks are stable and the complexity is considerable, this may be the only effective form. When work tasks change, due to changes in the context or the market, this form could be highly limiting.

Multidisciplinary Gestalt (integrated, higher level)

People from different disciplines bring ideas together creating a greater whole than they can do on their own. This process often depends on good dialogue and using each other's ideas as building blocks. A new, overall understanding emerges, a new Gestalt. In an integration like this, the actors from the different disciplines involved can see how their ideas fit within the whole. When the whole Gestalt emerges, the representatives for the different disciplines should be willing to modify or change their contribution in favour of the Gestalt. The outcome is a change in perspective on the value of one's own contribution.

Example: The goal is to contribute to ideas for how to recruit more blood givers. Communication people, medical workers and the Red Cross, work together and decide which of their discipline based ideas can be usefully employed to achieve the common goal. Given this activity, they form a new body of initiatives that reach out to new potential blood givers.

Theory: The Gestalt psychologists' most common quote is probably the saying that "The whole is greater than the sum of its parts". In leadership contexts, the metaphor of the bricklayer who either lays brick on brick, or builds a cathedral, is often used. This perspective is an invitation to the individual co-worker to see the whole and identify with a greater goal – and thus be motivated by something imaginary and prospective. To move between part and whole and see things from both within and without are shifts of level and points of view that can provide a new perspective on the ongoing conversation or activity. In organisations, leaders at higher levels will often have a greater possibility of seeing the whole. The choice of super ordinate models will have implications for the value of a subordinate's professional contribution.

Trans-disciplinary stage model (serial, project-stages)

The idea here is that ideas are relevant at different stages depending on where they are in the work process, e.g., starting, defining, ideas for solutions, executing etc.

Example: This occurs in project management, where different methods should be used in the planning and the execution phase. During planning, it may be relevant to use the Gestalt method mentioned above, while poly-disciplinary activities may be more appropriate in the execution phase.

Theory: The fundamental idea for phase division in project theories is tied to the necessity of adopting different mental models for work in the different project phases (Turner, 1993). In the creative problem-solving literature referred to above (VanGundy, 1981, 1987) distinctions are made between three dilemmas: alone or in group, focusing on understanding the challenge or on ideas for solutions, using open (diverging) and/or closing (converging) processes. A well-managed variation between these three dilemmas will often lead to a better and more creative management of open and creative projects.

The third form: When something pops up that is not logically connected

When working and being in dialogue with people holding different perspectives embedded in a good climate, we often experience that unrelated and expected ideas appear. This is due to the combination of the individuals' rich history of experience and interests that goes far beyond the interactive communication that is overtly taking place. Over time, people who work well together develop respect for each Other's work. Sharing of experiences and reflections leads to a better understanding of the Other's perspectives and challenges. This sometimes leads to a maturation of ideas at subconscious levels, ideas that are not relevant for the topic in focus, but relevant in the individuals' Other activities and understanding.

Example: Experience in the large group processes called Open Space, Future Search etc. – might give ideas for self-motivated discussion groups in LinkedIn (in these processes people are responsible for involving themselves in activities that they find motivating). Furthermore, this positive involvement can reframe possibilities for direct democracy.

Theory: In group processes in the 1960s, one was concerned with how Others could help a person to reveal some personal qualities otherwise repressed in the individual's conscious processes. The aim was that the feedback should lead to increased individual self-awareness. In creative group processes, the focus is not on individual learning, but on the knowledge made available within the group. This is especially relevant when the emphasis is on the tacit knowledge that underpins perception, language, values and practice. Tacit knowledge becomes explicit and accessible precisely through professionals voicing their views and perspectives in joint work experience.

In ongoing shared work this often occurs spontaneously and the process cannot easily be explained or planned ahead. Due to its emergent character, this process is often defined as radical. It is unpredictable and cannot be planned for. Within cross-cultural communication, surprise and provocation are seen as moments when new and totally different knowledge can emerge. Some, both practitioners and theorists, focus on the fact that a good dialogue where one truly learns about the Other's perspective, paradigms and dreams, is what provides the opportunity for new and different ideas of what is possible to achieve (Scharmer, 2007). This is also what happened in the case described at the beginning of this chapter. The family members' reformulation of their perspective of people in bureaucratic roles, led them into a new way of seeing Others and interacting with them. This was not an original intention in the process.

As described above, one of the challenges that initially triggered me was the lack of precision for how interaction patterns of ideas can convert into new knowledge. In my view these three descriptive basic forms shared above are good models that can be normatively applied in different settings. By normative I mean that as a facilitator you probe different ways of combining and applying perspectives. E.g. "Let us see and jointly evaluate this idea from an customer perspective (reframing)". "How can we let the customer take control of the service we deliver?" (change of power, new control regime). "How can we combine the most important suggestion from each stakeholder and make sure that we satisfy the implicit needs?"

I strongly advocate the importance of creating a shared understanding among everyone involved about what kind of structures and processes are in play at any given time. How else can each person know when and how to act in order to be a productive member of a team or organisation? Hopefully, this can lead to more precise facilitation and shared understanding of the interactive practices described above.

I have now suggested three different basic forms of how people can be involved in order to stimulate new knowledge through the interplay between ideas. Let me take a reflexive turn: Given these processes described above, what are the learning points for individuals, interdisciplinary interactions and cultural differences?

Personal level implications for creativity and innovation

First of all, it seems that the Diversity Icebreaker seminar creates a climate of psychological safety which is important for creativity and innovation in teams (Anderson & West, 1998; Edmondson, 1999). At the Hebrew University in Jerusalem, a group of researchers have experimentally measured effects of the Diversity Icebreaker seminar since 2012. In relation to creativity it has been documented that the seminar creates a climate of positivity, trust and tolerance that leads individuals to become more creative. The number of ideas was not the main criteria here, but rather increased novelty and complexity of ideas (Arieli et al., 2018).

Second, the Red, Blue and Green is about preferences in the way people like to treat information while working together in groups. The Greens easily come up with new ideas that bring the challenge to the table. They see opportunities, alternatives and suggest new ways of connecting ideas and people. The Blues are more concerned with analysing the situation, gathering data and making sure that reality is well described. They are practical and concrete and ask for the potential effect and impact of eventual changes. The Reds involve people through active communication and make sure that everyone is heard.

This model is a model of processes in contrast to perspectives. The illustration at the beginning of this chapter illustrates the idea that the first stage of creative problem solving, the divergent stage, is primarily a process that can be described as Green. The convergent stage is more Blue. The communicative functions that are needed for keeping both people and ideas connected is a Red process that is important at all stages.

Interdisciplinary implications for creativity and innovation

Creativity is about bringing new ideas into the game. Information and ideas are the building blocks. Knowledge is the connection or contextualisation in between ideas that are working in a way that creates meaning. Letting people in from different disciplines with different paradigms leads to a situation where both information, knowledge and meaning is colliding. The perspectives individuals bring forward lead to "moments of surprise" that create relevant new products and knowledge. This also allows the possibility of learning by looking retrospectively at the qualities of the paradigmatic components embedded in the disciplines involved.

I mentioned in Chapter 5 that the group processes embedded in the Diversity Icebreaker seminar have elements from three different science traditions, the natural sciences, social sciences and the humanities. The Diversity

Icebreaker seminar can be applied as an experiential exercise for creating a shared understanding of these scientific differences. This might also make it easier to think alternatively about reality, language and humanistic ideals. As a creative exercise these three different perspectives can be applied as a shared way of challenging dominant thinking in the creative process.

The implications of cultural differences for creativity and innovation

Cultural differences are significant for creativity and innovation in teams in at least two different ways.

First of all, the fact that cultures differ in the extent that they are open to change.

- Some cultures are more traditionally oriented than others with a more futuristic lens.
- Some cultures find it uncomfortable to live in uncertainty, which is an important element of the early stages of problem solving.
- Some cultures leave decisions to people in authority and are careful about taking risks and responsibilities.

The consequence of these differences means that the attitude and perception of what is good and bad differs very much in situations where groups of people from different cultures solve problems together. Being aware of this in creative and innovative processes makes it possible to plan to facilitate a workable interaction that embraces and acknowledges different individual starting points.

Secondly, ideas about what it means to work well together can be very culturally based.

- In some cultures, the focus on the individual is strong and in other cultures the dedication and loyalty to the group can dominate. This has implications for voicing new and radical ideas.
- In some cultures, adjusting interaction and work flows to exact schedules and deadlines is important and in others, social processes and interpersonal commitments may determine the time taken.
- Doing one thing at a time or doing many things at the same time varies systematically.
- Talking about private issues or not, creates different expectations concerning small talk and time spent.
- How and when you can appropriately give direct personal constructive feedback to whom, if at all, varies greatly across cultures, making it hard sometimes to manage group processes.

It can be useful to use the emerging differences across specific established cultural dimensions (as mentioned in Chapter 6) that could potentially cause, or are already causing conflict in any one group as the basis of a customised cultural value checklist exercise. Team members can be invited to anonymously mark their own preferences above a line, as well as what they think the norm is in the group below a line on a number of wall charts of scaled customised dimensions. This allows the team to instantly visualise and understand the spread of different expectations across any one of the dimensions in the checklist. They can then work through each dimension together and collectively agree workable ground rules around each key team dynamic such as leadership style, timeliness, making inclusive decisions, communication norms, giving feedback, resolving conflicts and whatever else is pertinent. Again like the reflexive part of the Diversity Icebreaker seminar, working through a customised value checklist means that often unconscious social team processes and different expectations are acknowledged, made conscious and shared early on in a psychologically safe space. The team learns how to manage differences in a positive non-personal context, supporting creativity and innovation (Canney-Davison & Ward, 1999).

Good advice

1   Create shared understanding of the norms of working together and integrating ideas across the different stages of creative problem solving.
2   There are different ways of playing with ideas such as to create new ideas. The three basic forms described can be applied as different approaches in order to search for new and integrated ideas.
3   Consciously communicating well across diversity is important, especially across different scientific disciplines.
4   Professionals have important elements of their identity linked to their own profession. Be aware that for this reason, conflicts on tasks can easily trigger personal emotions. Strong conflicts may lead to personal insecurity which means team members are less likely to have open minds to generate or embrace new ideas and change.
5   Psychological safety is important for people to voice their emerging and unique ideas.

Note

1   I published these ideas for the first time in a chapter in a book edited by H. Fyhn on interdisciplinary creativity (Ekelund, 2009). At that time I differentiated seven different forms, which in this presentation has been reduced to three forms. I collapsed three forms of interaction between forms into one, and three forms of pattern of interaction into the other. The last one is still kept as the last, now the third form.

Bibliography

Anderson, N.R. & West, M.A. (1998). Measuring climate for work group innovation: Development and validation of the team climate inventory. *Journal of Organizational Behaviour*, (19): 235–258

Arieli, S., Rubel-Lifshitz, T., Elster, A., Sagiv, L. & Ekelund, B.Z. (2018). Psychological safety, group diversity and creativity. Israel Organizational Behavior Conference. 3 January 2018. Tel-Aviv, Israel

Blakar, R.M. (1984). *Communication: A Social Perspective on Clinical Issues*. Oslo: Universitetsforlaget

Boyd, D. & Goldenberg, J. (2013). *Inside the Box. A Proven System of Creativity for Breakthrough Results*. New York: Simon & Schuster

Brannen, M.Y. (2004). When Mickey loses face. Recontexualization, semantic fit, and the semiotics of foreignness. *Academy of Management Review*, 29(4): 593–616

Canney Davison, S. & Ward, K. (1999). *Leading International Teams*. London: McGraw Hill

Dagestad, S. (2015). *Innovasjon i praksis, veien til den andre siden*. Oslo: Innoco

DiStefano, J.J. & Maznevski, M.L. (2000). Creating value with diverse teams in global management. *Organizational Dynamics*, 29(1): 45–63

Edmondson, A. (1999). Psychological safety and learning behavior in work teams. *Administrative Science Quarterly*, 44(2) (June): 350–383

Ekelund, B.Z. (2009). Håndtering av forskjellighet i team (Managing diversity in teams). In Fyhn, H. *Kreativ tverrfaglighet, teori og praksis* (pp. 182–205). Oslo: Tapir forlag

Habermas, J. (1981). *Theorie des Kommunikativen Handels. Band I und II*. Frankfurt am Main: Suhrkamp

Kuhn, T.S. (1962). *The Structure of Scientific Revolutions*. Chicago: University of Chicago Press

Luft, J. & Ingham, H. (1955). The Johari window, a graphic model of interpersonal awareness. *Proceedings of the Western Training Laboratory in Group Development*. Los Angeles: University of California

Maznevski, Martha L. (1994). Understanding our differences: Performance in decision-making groups with diverse members. *Human Relations*, 47(5): 531–535

Scharmer, C. Otto (2007) *Theory U*. Boston: Harvard Business School Press

Taylor, F.W. (1911). *The Principles of Scientific Management*. New York: Harper Row

Turner, J.R. (1993). *The Handbook of Project-based Management*. London: McGraw-Hill

VanGundy, A.B. (1981). *Techniques of Structured Problem Solving*. New York: Van Nostrand Reinhold.

Van Gundy, A.B. (1987). *Creative Problem Solving: A Guide for Trainers and Management*. New York: Quorum Books

Zaltman, G., Duncan, R. & Holbek, J. (1973). *Innovations and Organizations*. New York: Wiley

8   Promoting Blue efficiency

In 1994 I read a short presentation of an assessment named Team Climate Inventory in a UK based journal named People Management. *Michael A. West and Neil Anderson had created a 44 question inventory tapping into those team processes that were relevant for innovation in organisations. Together with two other professionals from Norway, we agreed to translate and promote the concept in Norway (Ekelund, Døscher & Taylor, 1996). Human Factors become the largest commercial user of the concept during the 1990s and we revised the application to make it more customer friendly (Ekelund, Jørstad & Maznevski, 2000). In this process of listening to customers and their challenges, one of my customer said: "Bjørn, most of the time our teams are not involved in creativity and innovation, but in delivering specific results defined by the organisation and market. How do we interact at best to support efficiency?" This comment made me aware that I had been fascinated by the "Zeitgeist's" focus on change. Moreover as consultants, we were happy to deliver models that helped organisations in areas where they did not have a long history. But, of course, teams and organisations spend most of the time producing pre-defined results, and have much less time for creativity and innovation.*

Introduction of a team model

Michael A. West was one of Europe's most experienced team researchers covering many areas of team dynamics. He described efficiency in teams while being most concerned about the team processes, rather than individual differences. It is clear from his work that the climate and practices for a team running with creativity is different from the climate and practices when the team goal is efficiency (Anderson & West, 1998). While common sense may suggest that homogeneity improves efficiency, in fact well managed diversity is also key to efficiency. The task is to utilise different preferences as well as specialised competencies and perspectives to best achieve the most output with least input.

Realising the need to understand efficiency, (being a very high Green myself) I started to form ideas for how the management of diversity can be customised to fit the differentiation of goals; e.g. creativity/innovation versus efficiency. I launched a model called Team Pyramid in 2005 (Ekelund &

Rydningen, 2008; Ekelund, 2009a/2015). In this chapter I will present a revised version of this Team Pyramid with a focus on efficiency. At the end of the chapter, I will explicitly relate this model to the three diversities at personal, interdisciplinary and cultural level. In next chapter I will expand this model of Team Pyramid when inclusive community, trust and collective identity are the overall goals. My ambition with this model has been to make good guidelines for how in practice, diversity can add more value than it costs. As such, it has been, since its inception, my evolving answer to a particular best practice of managing diversity in teams.

There are some important differences between the levels in this pyramid. The lower part of the pyramid shows the elements we think are absolutely necessary in order to make sure that diversity can lead to something good. This needs to be sorted out with all the team members involved in order to create a situation where all members can contribute to facilitative co-operative behaviour.

Why this involvement of everybody? If we are going to promote trust and the ability to improvise and problem solve, the members need to know each other's roles and capabilities. The next level shows two elements that boost motivation and strengthen the emotional bonding and sharing. The top of the pyramid is identified as collective reflection. At this stage, the team reflects together about its activities and ways of understanding its activities. This top box is one of the most important, and it is also challenging. It is challenging because a question is put forward that will trigger someone's ideas of not doing things well enough, even of doing them wrongly. And the imagination of this potential conclusion creates a feeling of uncertainty, shame and fear of blaming. For this reason, this stage is not something participants look forward to with joy. Avoidance behaviour, both individually and collectively, is a natural response. It is important to have

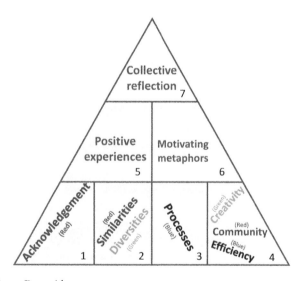

Figure 8.1 Team Pyramid

established a high degree of psychological safety and a positive learning culture in order to successfully enter this stage. I will elaborate more on these ideas as we look at the different stages in the pyramid.

Acknowledgement

I positioned Acknowledgement in the first box. This was in inspiration from my psychological background as a therapist, namely the Rogerian therapeutic tradition (Rogers, 1951). The therapist's unconditional acknowledgement provides a basis for safety, openness, self-reflection and movement. Similarly, for people working together across diversities, openness to Others as well as being acknowledged by the Others is a premise for interaction. What I also experienced in the inter-disciplinary work in the health sector was that inadequate acknowledgement leads to disappointment, deflation and repeated requests for being seen, heard and listened to. This blocked the openness for change and led to a lack of progress in teamwork.

Later on, I learned about Axel Honneth's perspective that he put forward in 1995 on the social philosophy of recognition. He states that the main conflict today in the world is the fight for being recognised (Honneth, 1995). His way of applying the word recognition is broader than the Acknowledgement term I use, but it overlaps and leads into the other elements of the pyramid. The recognition being sought is threefold. First of all, you have to be recognised as a valuable person per se with the right to speak up. Second, humans have not evolved as isolated individuals and for this reason you have a right to belong to a group. The forming of the group is an important part of the second box in the Team Pyramid. Third, you have the right to be recognised for your contribution and to see your contribution as contributing to something larger than yourself in a meaningful way. This is box number three and four in the Team Pyramid.

Honneth's work reinforced my experience in diverse teams on how the act of acknowledgement breaks down barriers, immediately settles any sense of uncertainty in team members about not being seen or heard as well as diffuses tensions between different expectations. It is a hugely important first step in creating the basis for efficiency in teams

Commonalities and differences

In the dynamics of teams, the focus on what you have in common and need to have in common and how you are different and need to be different are two seemingly opposing perspectives. In 2001, we introduced the Team Flower as a way of mapping the whole team. It becomes a model for creating an identity of the whole team, a shared mental model of the individuals, but made as a collective visualisation. Each participant receives a petal to show their own competence, values and preferences relevant for the team task.

The Team Flower as a graphic illustration gives the team members the possibility to fill the model with terms from different areas, not only the colourful dimensions, but also competence, network, attitudes, background etc. During the process, we ask every participant to share their own individual qualities, those they see might contribute to the team's creation of value. When everyone has shared the individual presentations, the centre of the flower is used to identify those concerns that are common for all. The petals show the collective heterogeneity needed to respond to complex problems, while the core of the flower shows what unites the team based upon what they have in common, the homogeneity. Diversity creates dynamics as well as the ability to respond to complex issues, while similarities, e.g. of shared common purpose and values, create feelings of belonging and trust.

Teams often keep this flower as a collective memory of such a mapping process. When a team member left, we were told, the person leaving received her or his petal, and the new team member was asked to fill in a new one. The new team member could look at the whole Team Flower to see how the individuals in the team described themselves in relation to each other in their defined relevant way. Then the new member could pick those elements from her or his background that are relevant to the others and the whole team. The Team Flower has the attractive quality that it gathers a picture of the whole team, made and understood together, it has a collective identity, while at the same time clarifying each individual's unique qualities. In some organisations, other metaphors or pictures are more appropriate than the metaphor of a flower. Gas turbines have sometimes been applied with the same illustrative function.

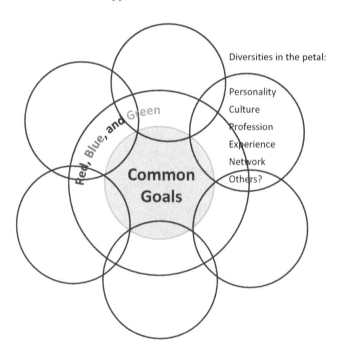

Figure 8.2 Team Flower

The common elements are very often shared purpose, goals, values and norms. These common elements become the unifying qualities that stand in contrast to the individual and differentiated descriptions in the petals. This image of a Team Flower is a social construction made into a shared picture. And there are some major different effects whether you focus on the different qualities in the petals or in the centre. If you focus on the centre, you focus on what you have in common. If you focus on the petals, you focus on the unique qualities, background, knowledge, experience and skills of each team member. If the team focuses too much on what they have in common, the team might end in groupthink. If they focus too much on what belongs to only one of the members, the group can fall apart. No team wants to be in any of these positions too long. Too much focus on diversity implies that the group can break apart, or into smaller subgroups, and activities can be difficult to coordinate and execute jointly. Too much focus on similarities may create a good climate of acknowledgment and belonging – but can lead to a certain blindfoldness. What we say is that a team needs to balance the two sides to succeed. The way I have presented the dilemma here, builds on the idea that it is the process of managing the focus that drives the team processes in opposite directions, such as the divergent and convergent processes described around problem solving in Figure 7.1 in Chapter 7. It is a question of maximizing the benefit of crafting and sequencing a rhythm of unifying and diversifying processes.

So it is not a question whether a team is "in reality" homogenous or heterogenous in a static compositional sense. All teams are both homogenous and heterogenous across different factors and dimensions. The Team Flower perfectly illustrates this. What is important is that independent of the heterogeneity in the backgrounds of the team members, the main question is what is in focus at any one time.

When focusing on what you have in common, you homogenise the shared mental and value based map of the team. One of the well-known key essentials of team success is ensuring clarity on the shared common purpose of the team from the beginning. This is the point of unity before focusing on using the diversified qualities and perspectives from each team member. When seeking to understand the problem by gathering multiple perspectives, then you are heterogenising the team, or "teaming" as some scholars have described it (Edmonson, 2012). However, when you heterogenise the team the interpersonal skills to integrate the ideas to a joint understanding are important. The shared understanding of Red, Blue and Green and a respectful interaction is an example of such interpersonal competence.

I find it very important to move away from the classical descriptive *nouns* of teams, which often leads to a rigid definition of a team, rather moving towards using process and emergent descriptions. When you homogenise you may create trust, harmony and commitment. When you heterogenise you often will do it for three main purposes: creativity, broad-based critical and analytical thinking, and distribution of tasks.

Processes: Defining our challenge, finding solutions, implementing and learning

In project management, the idea of making clear distinctions between different stages of the project process is a conceptual approach that is relevant for managing diversity in teams (Turner, 1993). As described in Chapter 7, in effective problem solving you need to have some time to analyse the problem, identify possible solutions, choose and implement them. An important part of the analysis is to share knowledge, perspectives and potential solutions. So this first stage is more intellectual, where working together effectively with ideas and communication is paramount, and the second stage is where effective coordination and sequencing of often individually performed tasks and activities is important. In this second active implementation stage the key is accessing and correctly allocating relevant expertise, competence and skill to ensure each sequenced task is completed in a timely way to the highest standard possible.

There are a myriad of books, tools and advice on effective project management. When initially jointly agreeing on the overall processes, at the core of all advice is how to go about answering the central questions of 'What are we doing together? Who does what, how, when to what purpose?

- The "who does what" is the identification of relevant individual qualities and competences. Reds will want to see that everyone is included and that their different knowledge and skills are equally respected and employed to the full. They will also want to ensure that ultimate success will be properly attributed to those who do the work and not co-opted by hierarchy. The Blues will look for details in the mapping and the clear assignment of tasks with delegated responsibility. The Greens will assure that the right people are on board to complete the full task.
- The "how" is important to make everyone aware of each others' activities in case there are some interface challenges between the different activities. For Blues, making an exact logical schedule and plan and seeing that everyone agrees to follow it and do their part will increase their trust in, as well as lower their anxiety about, the necessary agreed tasks getting done on time to the right standards. When this is in place they are more likely to be amenable to minor effective readjustments within the overall plan. Reds enjoy the interactive coordination and the feeling of being in cooperative teams. Green are impatient in their execution of tasks and might look for effective shortcuts.
- The "when" question is relevant in order to orchestrate stepwise elements in the planned activities as well as set the norms for different team activities at different stages. Blues have a natural tendency to show respect for deadlines and deliverables as promised. Reds can sometimes be too preoccupied by social commitments and expectations about taking part in other activities, and for this reason need to motivate themselves by respecting Others in the project and really deliver on time. For Green

people it is difficult, but important, to be aware that even the best ideas will not bring value if the timing is wrong. So for Green people the challenge is to know that many different ideas are useful at the first divergent stage of analysing the problem from different perspectives, and brainstorming possible solutions can add great value. However not introducing more good ideas during the convergent process of deciding which solution to go for, or during the action-oriented implementing stages of the project process, is the disciplined act that can bring the most value from Greens to the team. It is challenging for Greens to accept that they can add more value by being silent and not suggesting new ideas. But if the team gets stuck during these convergent and implementing stages, then for sure Greens can usefully add out-of-the-box creative ideas on how to get moving again.

Equally important to a common understanding of goals, roles and rules is knowing when to move on to the next phase, so that the individual's contribution is appropriate in relation to the process. Nothing is more annoying for a project manager in the performance phase than having people starting off every morning with new ideas about how things should be done. A shared understanding about the focus and norms at different stages will increase predictability by creating guidelines for everyone in a way that builds trust about what will happen in the future.

"Fit for purpose" efficiency

As mentioned earlier, teamwork is not only about promoting creativity and innovation, but also about working more efficiently. The question is how to utilise team members' individual competencies, their strengths, in order to have them involved with their particular areas of excellence. Efficient teams have identified their individual team members' strengths and weaknesses, and increased the efficiency by distributing responsibilities and duties accordingly. This is in practice an application of the administrative function as it was described by Frederick Winslow Taylor in 1911 in his book *Principles of Scientific Management*: the right man in the right place (Taylor, 1911). Shared understanding of how the different tasks will be executed in relation to the goal is important for each of the members of the team in order to be able to support each other and improvise together if unexpected problems occur.

Good collective experiences

Our observation is that having good experiences together makes people more dedicated and committed to the team. It creates more openness and positivity among members and leads to more interaction, flexibility and creativity. This leads to more knowledge about each other in the team, which is important for improvisation. Positive shared experiences build morale and increase the belief in the team's ability to reach its goals.

Reinforcing metaphors

Football is often used as a metaphor for teamwork. Another area of metaphors is music: singing in a choir, playing jazz and blues, being a member of a classical orchestra. Each metaphor has unique qualities that can reinforce motivation for teamwork. In soccer, there is a metaphor about "Best without ball", a metaphor that encourages the individual to act wisely even though you are not the one with the ball. You act in order to make others succeed by moving around, changing the form of the whole team, creating opportunities and disturbing players from the other team. You succeed as a helping guy. Such a metaphor reinforces helping behaviour in organisations.

One of the metaphors we appreciate very much is the making of French fish soup, Bouillabaisse. Not with the best French chef, but as a collective process inspired by "Barn-raising", or "Dugnad" which is the classical Norwegian term. It is a work process where individuals come together bringing the best materials and tools in a joint effort. All members have raw materials that are accepted in the soup. Following the making, sitting together, eating, participants starts recognising the individual taste of each component in the soup, asking each other "Who brought the beautiful carrots for this soup?" This is the acknowledging component that makes everyone sit together and take part in the whole meal. No one wants to leave before the meal is over. This is a metaphor that underlines the inclusive community which is the main focus in the next chapter. The "barn-raised bouillabaisse"-metaphor is a motivating image of teamwork that everyone appreciates.

Different organisational cultures use different metaphors to reinforce motivation and create meaning for individual roles. One of our clients uses team tours in the mountain where the team members plan together, distribute tasks, challenge the individual ideas of capabilities and make everyone improve their capability to reach their stretch goal inside the team's expedition project. Then afterwards, the leaders pull out elements from this shared experience as motivating metaphors for the individuals and the team. They have created a shared positive experience of achievement relevant for each person and for the group.

Collective reflection

Have we achieved our goals? What did not function well, and needs to be changed? How do we get back on track? What functioned well, and can this be strengthened even more? These questions are important in monitoring progress. In the quality literature, these questions have been thoroughly described in details with root analysis, action plans, etc.

The quality tradition has, as a starting point, deviation from goals and plans. Some people get really triggered by not achieving goals. Some people think that constant learning about failures and improvement is a personal challenge leading to important personal growth. But, it seems that many people find this negative focus on deviation demotivating. The focus on deviation very easily leads to the fear of being blamed and of not being good enough. The deviation per se often does not lead to clear answers about what to do better next time. Negative emotions and uncertainty about what to do is the consequence. For many people, this negative focus does not lead to positive motivation or learning how to do better next time.

An alternative model has gradually emerged over the last 20 years where appreciative inquiry (Cooperrider, 2005; Sørensen et al., 2010) and strength-based feedback (Rath, 2007) are two examples worth mentioning. Three central components in these interventions are i) to be more future oriented (Scharmer & Kaufer, 2013), ii) to focus on strength in the analysis more than weakness, and iii) the promotion of a positive feedback culture. It seems that these interventions as collective reflective processes open up the mind to more easily see new possibilities, build motivation for commitment to the group, and create energy for task performance. It seems that this approach for collective feedback creates more a shared feeling of hope for collective mastery.

Learning from failures and learning from success are both important collective feedback procedures. But, it seems important to be aware of the motivational consequences of the two different foci. Working with failures is the most challenging, because people are afraid of being seen as incompetent and blamed. That is why failures need to be managed thoroughly where positive elements count more than the negative ones. Highlighting a learning culture above and beyond the efficiency and performance oriented culture is helpful. But, learning does not fully take away the fear of being a failure. A compensating form might be to include reward mechanisms to areas of learning from failures as part of the management processes. Google is, among others, known for their monthly celebrating of this month's biggest failure. They say that the collective celebrating is a compensating form for explicit and implicit negative elements of doing wrong in organisations.

Case: Postal organisation with team feedback

In the postal organisation in Norway we trained team leaders to utilise the feedback from Team Climate Inventory (Anderson & West, 1998; Ekelund & Jørstad, 2002) to involve all team members to identify improvements on the following:

a   What has been our successes, and how can we strengthen those elements that have led to this success?
b   What shall we do differently in relation to areas with negative results?

Each team was asked to identify three actions in both areas mentioned above. The team leaders were trained to follow up the team's action plans in order to support their success. This involvement with leadership support showed clear improvement in all dimensions of the Team Climate Inventory (Ekelund, 2009b).

Personal level implications for efficiency

Red, Blue and Green describes preferences for how to use information while solving problems in groups. The different dynamics behind each colour play out most in the communicative and social interaction in the early analysis and brainstorming stages of problem solving. Later on, when execution is in focus, actions are less influenced by colour preferences if everyone is following the Blue implementation plan. It is also important to be aware that even if people have a predominant Blue preference, a preference for working with details, being practical, concrete and so on, it does not imply that they are competent at doing this. Preference is not the same as competence. People who have been able to choose activities that are aligned with their predominant preferences will probably have more practice combined with a positive attitude in this activity. Normally this will lead to a situation where the individual's competence is most developed aligned with individual preferences.

There are differences concerning what kind of work people prefer due to colour differences. And, it is probably right to expect people to have more motivation and stamina when they choose or when they have been given tasks in line with their preferences.

We have used Diversity Icebreaker to create sufficient psychological safety to be able to talk about individual differences. The positive climate that is created in the seminar promotes good dialogue. People report that it is easier to start giving each other feedback using the colour categories, as both the positive effect of the seminar is embedded in the colours as well as a non-personal approach. It can work very well with those from ethno-geographic cultures or within organisational contexts where direct personal feedback is not an accepted norm. When acknowledgement and group dynamics are managed well, there are fewer emotional tensions, making it easier for individuals to focus on their work.

Interdisciplinary implications for efficiency

Red, Blue and Green is about preferences, not competences. Education though, is a competence building capability that is important to take into consideration when tasks are distributed.

Working effectively in groups is not only a question of educated competence. Professional experience, knowledge about the Other members of the team, being acquainted with the organisational procedures and methods, network access and social competence for team work as well as effective communication are examples of competences that are important in order to succeed in interdisciplinary teams – and many of these are not prioritised inside professional education.

Acknowledgement of the Other as a competent professional is relevant for a person's feeling of acceptance and identity. In professional organisations, where pride and influence is connected with education and position, we see that an individual's identity is closely connected with the professional identity. Ignoring or insulting the individual's professional identity is often perceived as a threat to the individual's personal identity. This often leads to strong and only partially concealed grievance and a sense of not being recognised. Academic institutions have competitive disciplines that sometimes also display prejudiced and limited perceptions of the qualities of other professions. Meetings and communication between peers with similar professional background, for example in trade unions, might also lead to a reinforced polarisation between professions.

We often see participants in interdisciplinary teams feeling dissatisfied that they are not sufficiently understood on their own terms. When Other team members do not appreciate the positive and unique qualities one possesses and, instead, show disrespect, over-emphasising their own personal values, this leads to conflicts and unwillingness to participate in the team. We believe that one has to positively recognise the individual, as seen from the individual's own perspective, in order to establish a positive and flexible interaction between different participants.

The implications of cultural differences for efficiency

As discussed in Chapter 6, there is much implicit knowledge as well as lots of blind spots when people work across cultures. For this reason, knowledge about cultures, cultural intelligence, and being good at communicating is important for success.

As described above, cultural dimensions are expressions of important differences between people from different cultures. Cultural values are important for how individuals see and prioritise in their work life. There are more differences across cultures in relation to work life preferences than there are as compared with gender, age, level in the organisation and profession (Zander, 1997). This implies that the potential for "moments of surprise" is much higher in these settings than compared to more traditional diversity categories. Avoiding misperceptions and misunderstanding is for this reason of course one of the most important elements in the intercultural interaction.

In my focus on efficiency I have presented the Team Pyramid as an entrance to identify important success factors. I have focused very much upon interpersonal qualities and agreements between people working together in teams and projects. This fits quite well in cultures where loyalty to the working group is important and where individuals negotiate their own function with colleagues. In societies where leaders are more important, their activity is more important both in relation to acknowledgement of individuals as well as giving clarifying instructions for "who does what to which purpose". In some cultures delegation, discretion and trust are more prevalent, leading to a more proactive problem solving attitude among workers without involving leaders. In cultures where loyalty to the group is strong, involving all team members in defining goals, roles and rules can be more important. In some societies as well as working cultures there are stronger traditions around exact schedules and deadlines, while in other social systems flexibility and improvisation seem to be the most important qualities that lead to success.

Given all these cultural differences which are relevant for working together, the importance of acknowledging people and avoiding misunderstandings cannot be underestimated. In order to deliver efficiently it is also necessary to create shared agreements and commitments to contributions and deadlines in order to produce good quality results in time and at low cost. Lack of acknowledgement and misunderstandings derail this efficiency process. Early involvement and joint planning and learning and decision-making processes increase the possibility of success.

Connecting ideas

In this chapter I have focused on Blue preference for efficiency. Selecting the right goals and making sure that you apply resources in the right way is often a question of creative processes. If you want to ensure final success, you need to make sure that everyone delivers on their commitment to the team's goal. In many cultures, and so for Norway too, the loyalty to the working group, the team, is more essential than production goals. In such cultural contexts, involving all team members in goal setting as well as planning processes is important in order to succeed. People with Red, Blue and Green preferences have different elements that are important for loyalty and trust. More of this will come in the next chapter.

Good advice

1   Promote a culture of acknowledging the uniqueness of the individual as well as unique ideas. If people experience this in practice they will feel safer about showing more of themselves and voicing challenging ideas.
2   In all teams there are commonalities and differences. Homogenise and heterogenise at the right stages for the right impact while taking care of the group's needs.
3   Create a shared understanding about what we are coming together to do and why, who does what, when, how, and to what purpose.
4   The rules of the game are different when creativity and innovation is the goal compared to efficiency.
5   When feedback is given, make sure there is more positive than critical.
6   Role model being open about failures as well as successes.
7   Collective reflection is an important process for learning as well as building positivity.

Bibliography

Anderson, N.R. & West, M.A. (1998). Measuring climate for work group innovation: Development and validation of the team climate inventory. *Journal of Organizational Behaviour*, (19): 235–258

Cooperrider, D. & Whitney, D. (2005). *Appreciative Inquiry: A Positive Revolution in Change*. San Francisco: Bassett–Koehler

Edmonson, A. (2012). *Teaming: How Organizations Learn, Innovate and Compete in the Knowledge Economy*. San Francisco: Jossey Bass

Ekelund, B.Z. (2009a). Håndtering av forskjellighet i team (Managing diversity in teams). In H. Fyhn, *Kreativ tverrfaglighet, teori og praksis* (pp. 182–205). Oslo: Tapir forlag

Ekelund, B.Z. (2009b). Cultural perspectives on team consultation in Scandinavia: Experiences and reflections. *Scandinavian Journal of Organizational Psychology*, (2): 31–40

Ekelund, B.Z. & Jørstad, K. (2002). *Team Climate Inventory* – Intervention Manual. (Danish) Copenhagen. Danish Psychological Publication

Ekelund, B.Z. & Langvik, E. (Eds.) (2008). *Diversity Icebreaker: How to Manage Diversity Processes*. Oslo: Human Factors Publishing

Ekelund, B.Z. & Pluta, P. (2015). *Diversity Icebreaker II. Further Perspectives*. Oslo: Human Factors Publishing

Ekelund, B.Z. & Rydningen, M. (2008). *Diversity Icebreaker: Personal Workbook*. Oslo: Human Factors Publishing

Ekelund, B.Z., Døscher, H. & Taylor, R. (1996). TCI-presentation. *Norwegian Journal of Organisational Psychology* (Norwegian)

Ekelund, B.Z., Jørstad, K. & Maznevski, M. (2000). Business development of the Team Climate Inventory. *European Journal of Work and Organisational Psychology*, September: 9–18

Honneth, A. (1995). *The Struggle for Recognition. The Moral Grammar of Social Conflicts*. Cambridge: Polity Press

Rath, T. (2007). *StrengthsFinder 2.0*. New York: Gallup Press

Rogers, C.R. (1951). *Client-Centered Therapy. It's Current Practice, Implications and Theory*. Boston: Houghton, Mifflin

Scharmer, C.O. & Kaufer, K. (2013). *Leading from the Emerging Future. From Ego-System to Eco-System Economics*. San Francisco: Berret-Koehler

Sorensen, P.F., Yaeger, T.F., Savall, H., Zardet, V. & Bonnet, M. (2010) A review of two major global and international approaches to organizational change: SEAM and appreciative inquiry. *Organization Development Journal*, 28(4)(Winter): 31–39

Taylor, F.W. (1911). *The Principles of Scientific Management*. New York: Harper Row

Turner, J.R. (1993). *The Handbook of Project-Based Management*. London: McGraw-Hill

Zander, L. (1997). *The Licence to Lead*. An 18 Country Study of the Relationship between Employees' Preferences Regarding Interpersonal Leadership and National Culture. Dissertation IIB, Stockholm School of Economics

9 Promoting Red collective identity and trust

In 2002 I was, together with Sue Canney Davison, writing a chapter on managing global teams in Blackwell's Handbook of Global Management *(Lane et al., 2004). We tried to grasp how to work when people were recruited from all over the world, sometimes meeting face-to-face and often with e-mail communication. We were looking for concepts that could describe the individuals' feeling of belonging, belonging to a team that was globally distributed. "Emergent states" was a concept that came to our mind, a growing psychological feeling of being successfully connected, identified with the team, and producing results. We named this emergent state "collective identity". It became a concept that could overcome the lack of physical presence of teams in a locally situated organisation. Gradually we understood that this feeling of identifying yourself with the team due to being able to create more together than on one's own, was a feeling that also was important for members of locally situated teams.*

Since Sue and I both are very Green, we even formulated ideas that the "team" itself was only a mental construction. In reality a team is a number of individuals coordinating their work together. Even so, the feeling of being a team becomes an individual construct that presupposed the idea that others had similar ideas and were co-working together to produce results. Anyhow, after losing contact with the real world by chasing ideas, Sue and I gradually began to rephrase our thinking, and look for ways of eliciting processes that created a sense of collective identity that can interact with reality. In our ambitious Green dreams, we saw the potential of using the team concept for everyone in the world, and asked ourselves whether this could help people's willingness to accommodate to globally agreed constraints and different ways of going about things in order to save the planet from ecological disaster.

The emergence of Red values

The two previous chapters were about creativity and innovation, and efficiency; two different outcomes. At the end of each chapter I shared some starting ideas about how this could be applied in relation to individual/personal, scientific/paradigmatic and cultural/ethnic differences. The creativity and innovation path is about creating Green results. The efficiency path is mirroring the Blue quality. The last colour is Red, which is about inclusive community, a community where people identify with the group, where the psychological climate is dominated by trust and where ideas of succeeding as a team strengthen and are strengthened by the collective identification with the group.

As mentioned earlier, Red qualities are also important for both creativity and innovation, and efficiency. To present Red outcome variables as an outcome variable in its own right to be positioned along Green and Blue, is, for me, a relatively new way of presenting outcomes. When I presented the Team Pyramid in 2006, I focused on the major differences for teamwork dependent on whether achieving goals efficiently or creatively was the outcome variable (Ekelund & Rydningen, 2008). This was a hangover from the focus of my work with teams in the 1980s when bringing out more creativity was introduced as an important component in organisations. This aligned at the time with the changes in organisational strategies responding to the market changes that started in the 1970s.

Today, I think it is important to underline the importance of being together in a group, in an inclusive community. Positive identity, acknowledgement, good communication, trust and positive identification with the group are important examples of an inclusive community. They also allow a team to go above and beyond in many different ways. I think this shift of focus is important to highlight. Today, making new and better products and services has limited potential for creating increased happiness, positive identity, well-functioning economic organisations and democratic institutions. Red is about people, relations, feelings, trust and belonging. It is about psychological well-being, the subjective quality of life in contrast to material welfare.[1]

Red is important in and of itself. In my view, the Red qualities are important in every organisational setting. In corporate success and work-life, building on the "triple bottom line" goals – economic, social and the natural environment – is a way of building the capabilities of employees to act in a decent way in all settings. As mentioned earlier, in my view the training of employees and managers in work-life context has the potential to elicit "Bildung", the crafting and cultivating of self, in every person. Given our challenges, it is also important to strengthen the value of social interaction as an important contribution to psychological well-being and the quality of life.

As mentioned, in 2002 Sue Canney Davison and I wrote a chapter on global teams (Canney Davison & Ekelund, 2004). We followed up on Sue Canney Davison's work on international teams (Canney Davison & Ward, 1999). Differences in time zones, economic regulations in different countries and the underlying logic and use of language were among the many challenges faced by diverse teams. Additionally, Lena Zander had documented cultural differences as the most frequent major diversity issue. She gathered data in 18 European countries and found expectations of leadership varied the most due to cultural differences compared to gender, age, level in the organisation and profession (Zander, 1997). Sue Canney Davison and I decided to focus on two psychological factors: "collective identity" as mentioned at the beginning of this chapter, and "trust". We saw these two factors as psychological emergent states that we could treat as outcome variables emerging simultaneously, with the team producing tangible real task-based results. We thought these were good intermediary factors that could promote and predict success in multicultural teams.

Today I think these factors are factors that stand out as goals in themselves, as a proxy to the concept of "inclusive community", a term that reflects the tangible sense of belonging to a group. They include the personal satisfaction due to being acknowledged and the pride of being able to collectively cope with important challenges. For me, this is Red doing its work in a group. Liv Cardell in Sweden has defined this as Red Matters – a project to highlight the human oriented values in teams and organisation (Cardell, 2015). Red qualities are not a means to another end, but can stand for themselves as one of the goals we should strive for as homo sapiens.

I will start this chapter by sharing the theoretical and empirical learning that I have been involved in around trust and collective identity. I will use these two factors as a starting point for developing a better understanding of what a Red Inclusive Community is about. Then I will end this chapter by going back to the personal, scientific/paradigmatic and cultural differences, and how they can add value to this goal.

Theoretical perspectives on inclusive community, trust and collective identity

What is an inclusive community?

To belong to a group is something a person feels, an emergent state, and it is something that is seen in practice by shared organised acts and inclusive communicative behaviour. I have pointed out earlier how some categories within language can function as excluding, like gender, race, profession and more, and how in comparison, the categories of Red, Blue and Green include everybody at the collective level. At the same time, it is about the integration of individuals, as well as their making a contribution that is recognised as important to something bigger than themselves (Honneth, 1995). It is going from the psychological feeling and question of the individual – "Am I included or not?" – to inclusive communicative practices that lead to coordinated and integrated activities.

Norway is a country on the outskirts of Europe, with some elements of wealth, democracy and equality making it into one of the more attractive societies in the world. Let me look at Norway as a laboratory for trust and inclusiveness. And, then use my participation in this society as an innovative organisational psychologist trying to push borders to understand what are central elements of collective identity and trust.

How do I envisage what is important for being included? From 1995 onwards I have gathered data and developed assessment models around individuals and team climates for innovation and performance.[2] Climate in teams and organisations is defined in this context as shared perceptions (Anderson & West, 1998). In 2005, I had an opportunity to revisit some of my empirical research work on individual perceptions and team climate in a one week training program in Denmark on advanced statistical analysis that combined individual and team levels in hierarchical linear models. At the end of the week, I imagined a journalist asking me; "Given all the data and analysis you have from Norwegian teams; with you being a Norwegian, what recommendations will you give in order to make teams successful as seen from the individual team member's point of view?"

My answer was "Ask each person for ideas for how things can be best done, listen to what they suggest, integrate their ideas into the solution, and invite them to take part in the execution." This answer represents three important aspects. To ask for advice is a validation of the member's unique potential contribution. This is a practical acknowledgement of the individual's worth. Integrating the idea into the solution, in practice, is showing that you belong and that your words are valuable in the work we will do together. Making sure that you contribute in the execution integrates the individual and collective communication into practical action. A successful outcome for the team will confirm the value of the whole process and reinforce the importance of the individual, as well as the inclusive team process.

This short recommendation illustrates Axel Honneth's (1995) work on recognition. As a social philosopher, he asks what kind of norms we need in order to live together in a society. As mentioned earlier, his answer is "Recognition" of the individual due to the individual's needs: Each person has a right to be listened to, be a member of a group and contribute to something larger than him/herself. My recommendations for the inclusive work the team can do are aligned with these ideas. And, I will use these perspectives as the core elements in an inclusive community.

What is trust?

What are the important qualities of trust when a diversified group of people are solving problems together, in particular, when the diversities are personal, interdisciplinary and culturally based?[3]

Trust has been defined in many different ways. It is normally defined as "being treated well by Others when you are vulnerable". There are three main factors in trust:

i   vulnerability,
ii some Others with power to influence,
iii and the person in power using his/her influence to care, help, and be considerate towards the person who is vulnerable.

(Whitener et al., 1998; Hua et al., 2003)

In groups where diversities are spelled out, we can surmise various groups of people who may feel vulnerable for different reasons:

- People who belong to a minor group with little prestige.
- Those who for whatever reason have not delivered as expected and are concerned about negative sanctions.
- Those who voice concerns that threaten the main logic in the organisation or the people in power.

So this is, one might say, a type of trust that focuses on the interaction between people, where vulnerability and power are the important qualities.

There is also a type of trust that can be developed between people at an equal level. This happens when you both perceive that you share the same values, norms and goals; a kind of value alignment. Being together with people like yourself makes you feel safe. You trust people like yourself since you expect that you have comrades in critical situations, comrades that you expect will act in line with yourself and not threaten you in critical situations.

The extent and quality of someone's loyalty to the group is also a central question in how much you trust and are trusted by another person inside the group. Without loyalty, there is no bonding that prevents the other from leaving the group when opportunities are better in another place. Loyalty may be in part a consequence of positive relations and reciprocal interests. Being personally acknowledged as valuable for the group will foster the development of a positive identity and give individuals good cards to play in give-and-take interactions.

The belief that the community has better problem-solving capabilities and/or opportunities by staying together might also be a good reason for belonging and acting in line with the group. The group has the capacity to deliver more than the individuals (Ekelund & Moe, 2014). If the group represents a positive quality – either in competence, recognition in society or other aspects – it is attractive to be a member of that group, and the identification and inclusion will increase an individual's positive self-image. Confidentiality is a group norm for teams, a norm that makes it easier to share vulnerable stories. Sharing vulnerabilities and being treated well by Others in the team leads to a situation of interpersonal debt and expectancy of reciprocity. For example, if I do not know what to do and Others help, I will look for opportunities to return the gift given.

Predictability of processes is a component of trust that is different from the above. Predictability is about knowing what will happen, and how things will proceed. An expectation of fair treatment is an example of trust that motivates people to move forward. Knowing that conflicts will be managed in a discrete and confidential way is also an element of predictability in vulnerable situations. Predictability concerning everyday routines, meeting structures, decision making and traditions are also elements that, at a less critical level, create a basic structure of stability, which make it easier to improvise when needed.

Shared destiny is also something that increases loyalty to the group. The ecological crisis is not something that can be solved by individuals alone. The ecological crisis has a potential of bringing all people together in a joint effort.

The way I have described trust above links the concept to the individual's feeling of being vulnerable, a feeling I assume is central for minority people as well as for people who have a concern that their presence and contribution may not be well received in the group or the community. I have further built trust as something going deep into the quality of interaction with Others, with and without power differences, deep into the group, strengthened by predictable structures and the idea of shared destiny towards future challenges. Trust is in this way, contextualised as a broad and central quality for individuals and groups addressing important challenges, where the intention is to create a practice of including minority perspectives in collective decision making and actions.

What is collective identity?

Collective identity is about the individuals that relate to and identify with the group. The identification may be due to the tightly interwoven history of shared experiences which has created bonds between the people in the group and the group itself. It can be strengthened by conflicts with Other groups or by having come through a conflict or difficult situation together as a group. Also important in contributing to collective identity and "team glue" are:

- Shared destiny
- An alignment of values at least the basic values and overall goals
- The expectancy of being included in decision making as well as equitable and fair processes for managing conflicts and distributing task
- Being treated well by the Others in the group

These elements that contribute to collective identity very much overlap with the components of trust described at the beginning of the chapter. This indicates that important words and categories represent different perspectives that bring light to similar phenomena. The phenomena of an "emergent state" of feeling trust inside a group of people, is where shared values are important for creating commonality, and simultaneously diversity is applied to differentiate roles in order to achieve a complex shared goal. It is what is called Diversity & Unity at the same time, or in a more process oriented language, diversifying and unifying at the same time (Matoba & Ekelund, 2013).

In 2003, I created an interdisciplinary checklist of 12 factors in order to study team members' experience in interdisciplinary team contexts. The factors are different in character and combine issues from organisational theory, group processes and management of teams. The 12 factors are organised into three main categories with the following subcategories:

- Input: Goals, responsibility, rules and roles
- Processes: Team leadership, meeting structure, communication, decision processes, managing diversity, reflection and learning and conflict management
- Output: Trust and collective identification

"Collective identity" was defined in line with the theoretical work that was described from a global team perspective (Canney Davison & Ekelund, 2004). The underlying similarities with cultural values and scientific paradigms outlined earlier is the reason why I chose to transform this theoretical work into the area of interdisciplinarity. In the "collective identity" factor, the initial question concerns the sense of community and pride in the team. The next question concerns each person contributing, thus giving all the team members a feeling of being integrated. After this, a question is asked whether one can see that the team is producing better results as a consequence of collaboration. The final question is about the extent of recognition received from external sources.

"Managing diversity" is another process factor in this interdisciplinary checklist that is very relevant for the problems addressed in this book. The items for this factor concern whether the team members find it positive to contribute with perspectives and suggestions typically anchored to their own discipline and whether these are being received with acknowledgement and respect from the Others. To what extent do the team members feel they know how to interact on the basis of the different disciplinary perspectives? Also included is the degree to which the team climate actually invites the individual to share unique disciplinary and professional perspectives, specific for this competence area and tradition. Finally, one item explores whether teamwork is perceived as contributing to their own professional development inside their own discipline. In this factor in the interdisciplinary checklist, you recognise elements described above from an inclusive community. At the same time, it adds the idea that individuals should experience some positive growth in their own discipline due to interdisciplinary teamwork.

Are homogenous or heterogenous teams better at creating inclusive communities?

In the literature on cultural diversity in teams, there have been some models around successful and unsuccessful teamwork that have a generic quality. After introducing these concepts, I will share analysis of the data from the interdisciplinary checklist which challenged these models. Nancy Adler suggested that heterogenous teams will either perform better or worse than homogenous teams (Adler, 1991).[4] Joseph DiStefano and Martha Maznevski (2000) suggested calling the heterogenous teams that tipped in a positive direction "Creators" and those going in a negative direction "Destroyers". Teams that suppressed the heterogeneity were named "Equalizers". What they all stated was that in relation to heterogenous teams, the quality of management was the factor that decided whether the team ended up being a "Destroyer" or "Creator". As you can see we are still compiling the best practices for becoming "Creators" who make the most of diversity as mentioned in Chapter 1.

As far as I know these ideas have not been confirmed outside student samples (Watson et al., 1993). In my work with the checklist, I had 643 responses from people working in very heterogenous teams as far as professional disciplines are concerned, namely small groups of employees from different health disciplines, working and delivering a breadth of health services. I had data on diversity management – which I treat here as an important factor of an indication of "being led well". I had data on "collective identity" which could be applied as an outcome variable. I asked myself the question "Would it be possible to empirically validate the categories described by the researchers mentioned above?" I defined what I called Low, Medium and High on diversity management. The graphical results indicate similarities to the model described by Adler, DiStefano and Maznevski.

In Figure 9.1, the first group of bars illustrate the groups that are low on diversity management and named "Destroyers". The middle bars represent the groups that are medium on diversity management and named "Equalizers". The bars at the right are the groups that are high on diversity management and named "Creators".

In response to the question whether I could identify the categories of "Destroyer", "Equalizer", and "Creator", the answer was "Yes". But, there were two other discoveries.

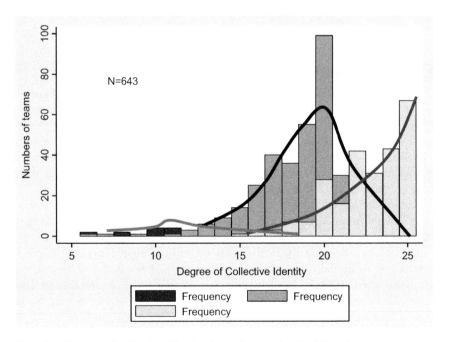

Figure 9.1 Degree of collective identity dependent on level of diversity management

First of all, the "Creator" teams seem to increase exponentially in the graphical illustration. Their distribution did not have the normal Bell-distribution curve like the two others. This can be explained by the fact that we analysed individual perceptions and did not use mean scores for all members in the team. For some individuals working in very good teams, often named high-performance teams, they may have felt it right to score absolutely maximum. But, it is unlikely that we would get absolute top score if we had used the mean of all members of the team since some members would have scored lower, even though they were in a good team.

Second, the teams that scored in-between low and high on "diversity management" created a beautiful Bell-curve, a normal distributed curve. But, this group is not homogenous – but still it looks like the homogenous group in the model. How come? Given what I know from my work with this field, and in line with the qualitative data reported by DiStefano and Maznevski (2000), my best hypothesis is that they suppress the interdisciplinary conflicts and focus on things they can agree on, things they have in common. I suggest calling the process of repressing conflicting ideas "homogenisation". These results give good reason to suggest a hypothesis that there are different dynamic processes inside heterogenous teams that lead to different group results. And when I did regression analysis inside each of the empirically defined groups of "Destroyers, Equalizers and Creators" I found different components predicting success inside each of the groups. Among "Destroyers", conflict management was important. Among the "Creators" team leadership was important. Among the :Equalizers" most activities you find suggested in team books were relevant (Ekelund, 2009).

Trust in the Scandinavian context

In this book I have clearly stated that is written with a cultural background called "made in Norway" at the same time as I am relating to challenges that are globally relevant. In order to see and understand the results in the context where it has evolved, and in order to see opportunities and limitations for dissemination of practice, it is important to clearly spell out the elements in Norwegian culture that are relevant for an inclusive community and in particular for trust and collective identity.

Norway has a government led welfare state that takes care of people's needs independent of background in relation to school, health and social services. People know they will be taken care of if they are unlucky, unhealthy, not competent, etc. People trust that the system, and the people working in public systems, are dedicated to the goal of serving people in the best way, that people get help when needed. Trust in bureaucracy and other institutions of civic society is large. The World Values Survey indicates Norway as one of the highest ranking societies concerning high trust (http://www.worldvaluessurvey. org/wvs.jsp). The value of societal trust is estimated to be at the same level as the fund established following our taxation of oil exploitation (Cappelen,

2017). The propensity to trust measured at individual level is about one standard deviation higher than the USA and UK (Nordvik, Berg & Ekelund, 2000). The general belief is that human beings are basically good which implies that we start by trusting people, and they need to break that trust in order to earn distrust. In many other societies you have the opposite process; you have to act and be seen to be trustworthy before you earn trust. In Norway, to include everybody seems more important than focusing on selecting only individuals with good competences and success. One of our most popular tunes that everybody across generations knows in Norway, starts "You will get another day tomorrow, where you start again". If you are unlucky, you will always get a second chance. The conclusion is that Norway is a high trust society that takes care of people when they are vulnerable.

Personal level implications for inclusive community

As mentioned in previous chapters, the language of Red, Blue and Green diversifies at the individual level. We focus on the primary preference that makes you stand out compared to Others. At the same time, each colour seems to be defined as a contrast to the other, leading to a quality of differentiation yet complementarity. When complex problems need to be solved, all the colours are important, with different perspectives and different roles, both in communication, problem solving and execution. The language itself diversifies individuals and unifies at the collective level (Matoba & Ekelund, 2013).

Research at Hebrew University in Jerusalem has documented that the Diversity Icebreaker workshop reduces distrust and creates positive effects (Arieli et al., 2018). The humour in the workshop seems to make individuals feel alike and as such it contributes to the attractiveness of being in the group (Pluta, 2015). The humour facilitates reflection (Bergson, 1911) which is an important part of a team's ability to be innovative and solve problems (West, 2000). Qualitative research on people's experience in the use of Red, Blue and Green indicates that the colourful categories make people feel more competent in giving feedback and solving problems with less personal conflicts (Ekelund et al., 2015). A title from a conference in Finland illustrates this: "Reframing Others in Colours of Mastery" (Ekelund & Pluta, 2017). People want to be a member of a group which can solve problems in a better way. In order to solve Grand problems, we need groups that are considerably better at solving problems and include many more very divergent starting points at a different order of magnitude.

As I have emphasised in previous chapters, when we run the Diversity Icebreaker seminar, the participants experience the positive feeling of being together with people who share the same preferences. Later on, they often develop an easiness about how they characterise themselves and Others, also applying more negative and even insulting words. Then, when the groups share what they have written about each Other, they see that they all have in common potentially tough and negative descriptions of the Others. People present the negative descriptions with self-irony and humour, well aware that these are words reflecting their own stereotypes more than necessarily generic qualities of the Other. When everyone shares this experience with humour, we see a feeling of collective relief. This happens without people being excluded due to what they say. We assume that this quality leads to more social openness about the darker qualities of personal attributes without fear of being excluded. It might explain why people say it is easier to give negative feedback (Ekelund et al., 2015) and why participants more easily give voice to ideas about organisational improvements (Rubel-Liefschitz et al., 2014) in the Diversity Icebreaker seminar.

When we ask participants what they have learned, one of the most typical comments is: "We see we can create good outcomes if we can acknowledge each Other and synergise working together. We need someone with ideas, that is, Green in action. We need someone to keep people together with trust and openness. That is a quality much appreciated by Red. And we need someone to structure our work and lead execution, and Blue is the preferred quality in that stage." Blue, Red and Green are concepts that naturally constitute themselves as complementary, necessary and dependent on each other. They are elements that lead to some kind of Gestalt. This quality of the concepts makes it easy in seminars to discuss premises for how diversity can create synergy. Each element is needed to create the total picture. Diversity becomes a part of the Gestalt.

Do Red, Blue and Green people have different values concerning what contributes to trust? We saw that the result of empirical analysis of interdisciplinary teams illustrates different processes that lead to trust. Some of these qualities have qualities that align with the attributes of particular colours. "Rules and regulations", the predictability of processes, we think, are more relevant for Blue people. "Managing diversity inclusively" is probably more relevant for Red people. "Collective reflection" is what we assume that Green people find important. These are our assumptions, to be researched later.

Interdisciplinary implications for inclusive community

As illustrated before, interdisciplinary teams are exposed to individuals with strong professional self-identities. The need to acknowledge the value of the Other, aligned with their own value systems and competence, is important. A shared and positive understanding of each other's unique qualities is necessary in order to establish interaction between individuals where these qualities become accessible for collective utilisation. To create a common ground, a shared platform, where commonalities and diversities are expressed, is important.

To achieve a shared platform where problems can be solved, one has to create a climate where knowledge across disciplines can be shared and contribute to the development of new solutions. Von Krogh and colleagues describe *Ba* as a good learning environment when knowledge creation is important (Krogh, Ichijo & Nonaka, 2000). "*Ba* is essentially a shared space that serves as a foundation of knowledge creation, one that is often defined by a network of interactions." Knowledge development makes special demands for relationships in order to succeed. Von Krogh et al. say that in *Ba* five dimensions of care among people are important: *Mutual trust, active empathy, access to help, courage and no condemnation* (Krogh, Ichijo & Nonaka, 2000: 69). Care is seen as a continuous process and evolves through strengthening these capabilities both at the individual and collective level.

The implications of cultural differences for inclusive community

One of the main differences between cultures is the dimension of individualism. This is an idea that has emerged in western European cultural history through the Renaissance. It was the time period in western history where leading persons formed the idea of the importance of the individual. Later on, the growth of democracy strengthened the individual's right to vote and take part in national and local issues. And, then in the last century, the declaration of human rights solidified the respect of the individual in relation to the community and systems of power.

The mainstream ideal of western European societies today is a deliberative democratic society, where individual rights are protected and lived fully, and where democratic systems solve collective challenges, with independent judiciaries separated from religious institutions. Many other societies have sometimes very different or only slightly nuanced different ways of solving these issues that are not aligned with western European ideas. These range across many factors such as the right of all citizens to vote in multiparty elections after a certain age, whether women or men; limited terms in senior office, the role of religion, freedom of speech, rights of abode and citizenship, and many more. One of the ideas inherent in creating sovereign national states has been that each state has some rights to solve their problems in the way they choose inside their own borders. The problem with, for instance, the climate crisis is that it does not respect man made borders and the lack of satisfactory solutions within many countries leads to a situation where people move in large groups. The number of detained people, according to the UNCHR, has increased tremendously. The Syrian crisis, resulting in many refugees entering Europe, has triggered a situation where the capacity, competence and willingness to integrate people from another region and culture has been challenged.

This book is written from a Norwegian background and context and in line with the importance of creating cultures and systems where individual and group voices outside the established systems/people in power are heard with respect and dignity. When we receive immigrants through the borders and walls/fortress of Europe, how do we meet these people in an inclusive way, with trust and make them a part of a society to which they belong, feel proud of, and can identify with?

In political discussions, these questions are more important today and many different initiatives are happening within refugee camps. These include integration programs where refugees are settled, benefit from language training, housing, competence credentials being transferred from source to host country, mentoring programs in industry for work employment. In some of these areas Diversity Icebreaker has been tried out in Norway, Serbia, Greece, Germany and the USA in the development and training of both employees and refugees/ immigrants. This has just started and further experiences and research will be sought out.

Case: Middle East

Another alternative to working with migration issues is to stimulate a better situation in areas that are in deep conflict and where people seek to get out. Norway has a tradition of giving aid and helping in peace processes. Inspired by the same attitude I started out in 2011 to pursue the idea of applying Diversity Icebreaker in the war inflicted area of Israel and Palestine (Ekelund, 2013/2015). I wanted to see how the concept could add value there. Another goal was that I wanted to learn with competent local people how such a concept could be applied in a totally different cultural and con-flictual context. In the last partly crowdfunded project, I had the opportunity of working with the largest peace organisation in Israel and with universities in Palestine that train students in conflict management. A model of how the Diversity Icebreaker contributes as a trust builder in these areas was for-mulated out of the first experiences. These experiences also influenced important ideas of norms and values of dignity that are central in the next chapter. The model presented in 2013 looks like the following.

In this model, Figure 9.2, the left first box (1–5) highlights the qualities we see in the Diversity Icebreaker seminar. The upper box (6) marks the con-tinuity of these ideas, a continuity of participants' expectancy of acting along with the positive experiences from the Diversity Icebreaker seminar – a continuity and positive expectation that creates trust in processes in the future. The right middle boxes (7–8) are emotional and cognitive collective products that reinforce the positivity and continuity of the collective learning. The box at the bottom (9) is the one that people from the Middle East put forward to reflect their reality, a reality that did not come to my mind coming from a peaceful and trustful society like Norway.

Connecting ideas

In this chapter I present how, beyond creativity/innovation and efficiency, I have stressed the issue of feeling as if you belong to a group, of being included and valued. Inclusiveness at a collective level is the Red outcome that is important in order to create and further develop civic societies. I have stressed that this perspective is an important added value to the traditional goals in organisations. This will be even more important when Grand questions,

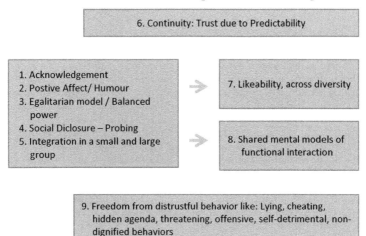

Figure 9.2 Trust model

ecological crises and large groups of people escaping to other countries are testing our borders for humanity. I ended this chapter by referring to my work in the Middle East. Africa is one of the continents where Diversity Icebreaker seminars have been executed and 5 of them are summarised in a paper presented in Nairobi in 2016 (Canney Davison et al., 2016). In the dialogues following this presentation a question was raised that needs to be answered. What are the Red qualities in African contexts that can be exported as inspiration and guidance for the western world? More research with qualitative methods is one of our scopes for the future. In the next chapter I will share examples of the application of Diversity Icebreaker in contexts where doing Good is central.

Good advice

1   The feeling of belonging to a group, being included and valued are essential qualities and a legitimate goal in organisations and societies. Make sure that you see, listen and hear Others and include them in real productive work.

2   Trust is about being treated well by Others, equality, loyalty, predictability and shared destiny. Use all elements to build and solidify the climate of trust.

3   Diversify, but do not forget to unify at the same time. Be aware of how different categories and ways of communicating include and exclude.

4   The Diversity Icebreaker seminar has trust-building capabilities that also seem to function across cultures.

5   Be aware that Norway/Scandinavia is a high trust society. For this reason it is a story to be inspired by, although one not easily replicated in other cultural settings.

Notes

1 In 1983 I delivered my thesis in psychology at University of Oslo on subjective well-being. At this time there was huge interest in developing an alternative measure to Gross National Product (GDO). The relative low connection between material wealth and happiness triggered the search for alternative answers. I looked for what elements that statistically could predict subjective well-being. First of all it was nearest family, second friends and at third level it was work. For me, it was a confirmation of the importance of social aspects as a contrast to material wealth.

2 In 1995 I started to map team climate based upon the Anderson & West (1998) TCI model (Team Climate Inventory). In 2003 together with Michael A. West I constructed an assessment forTeam Perfomance. In the same year I made an assessment for interdisciplinary teams. More than 4,000 teams have been mapped with these models through the company of Human Factors between 1995 and 2018. Both theoretical models, empirical results and consultative work based upon these models have given me foods for thoughts in the development of Diversity Icebreaker applied in teams and organisations.

3 I have researched and written about trust in many different contexts. First time in relation to leadership across cultures (Hua et al., 2003), different sources of legitimacy across cultures (Smith et al., 2003), consequences of breaching psychological contract in different cultures (Thomas et al., 2010), in interdisciplinary teams (Ekelund, 2009) and in management teams (Ekelund & Moe, 2014).

4 Nancy Adler (1991) and Joseph DiStefano and Martha L. Maznevski (2000) focus on cross-cultural differences in their books and articles. But, the model on managing diversity is treated here due to the similarity of challenges of managing diversities independent of diversities due to cultural differences, scientific paradigms or personal differences. This is in line with what is written earlier in this book, but also in the chapter I wrote with Joseph DiStefano in 2002 (DiStefano & Ekelund, 2002).

Bibliography

Adler, N.J. (1991). *International Dimensions of Organizational Behavior*. Quebec: McGill University Press

Anderson, N.R. & West, M.A. (1994). *Team Climate Inventory: Manual and User's Guide*. Windsor, Berkshire, UK: NFER-Nelson

Anderson, N.R. & West, M.A. (1998). Measuring climate for work group innovation: development and validation of the Team Climate Inventory. *Journal of Organizational Behaviour*, (19): 235–258

Arieli, S., Rubel-Lifshitz, T., Elster, A., Sagiv, L. & Ekelund, B.Z. (2018). *Psychological Safety, Group Diversity and Creativity*. Israel Organizational Behavior Conference. 3 January. Tel-Aviv, Israel.

Bergson, H. (1911). *Laughter: An Essay on the Meaning of the Comic*, C. Brereton and F. Rothwell (trans.), London: Macmillan

Canney Davison, S. & Ward, K. (1999). *Leading International Teams*. London: McGraw Hill

Canney Davison, S. & Ekelund, B.Z. (2004). Team processes in global teams. In H. Lane, M. Mendenhall, M.L. Maznevski & J. McNett (Eds.), *Handbook of Global Management. A Guide to Managing Complexity*. (pp. 227–249). Hoboken, NJ: Blackwell Publishing

Canney Davison, S., Ekelund, B.Z.Gjerde, S.Boodhun, V., Guttormsgard, I., Malde, Y. S., Handeland, A.Dahlmann, O.P., Gyan, K.A. , Dybwad, A.Johnston, K., Fjell, K. &

Lane, H. (2016). Trainer Experiences Applying Diversity Icebreaker in 15 African Countries. Presented in Nairobi, Kenya, at the African Academy of Management, 8 January 2016

Cappelen, A. (2017). Trust is more valuable than our oil. https://www.forskningsda gene.no/artikler/tillit-mer-verdt-enn-oljen-vr!t-724

Cardell, L. (2015). *Red Matters*. Malmö: Cardell Consulting

DiStefano, J.J. & Maznevski, M.L. (2000). Creating value with diverse teams in global management. *Organizational Dynamics*, 29(1): 45–63

DiStefano, J. & Ekelund, B.Z. (2002). Management across cultures. A model for bridging the differences. In M. Fladmark (Ed.), *Heritage and Identity: Shaping the Nations of the North* (pp. 289–304). Shaftesbury: Donhead

Ekelund, B.Z. (2009). Håndtering av forskjellighet i team (Managing diversity in teams). In H. Fyhn, *Kreativ tverrfaglighet, teori og praksis* (pp. 182–205). Oslo: Tapir forlag.

Ekelund, B.Z. (2013) Diversity Icebreaker applied in conflict management from Norway, through the Balkans to the Middle East. SIETAR Europe Conference in Tallinn, 20 Sept 2013. Presented in B.Z. Ekelund & P. Pluta (Eds.) (2015). *Diversity Icebreaker II. Further Perspectives*. Oslo: Human Factors Publishing

Ekelund, B.Z. & Langvik, E. (Eds.) (2008). *Diversity Icebreaker: How to Manage Diversity Processes*. Oslo: Human Factors Publishing

Ekelund, B.Z. & Moe, T. (2014). Team leadership in community childcare (Norwegian). In Ø. Kvello & T. Moe, *Barnevernsledelse*. Oslo: Gyldendal

Ekelund, B.Z. & Pluta, P. (Eds.) (2015). *Diversity Icebreaker II. Further Perspectives*. Oslo: Human Factors Publishing

Ekelund, B.Z. & Pluta, P. (2017). *Reframing Others in Colours of Mastery*. Nordic Intercultural Communication Conference, 23 Nov. 2017. Jyväskylä, Finland

Ekelund, B.Z. & Rydningen, M. (2008). *Diversity Icebreaker: Personal Workbook*. Oslo: Human Factors Publishing

Ekelund, S. M., Brannen, M.Y., Brannen, N.C. & Ekelund, B.Z. (2015). A trajectory theory of language development in organizations following Diversity Icebreaker seminars. Presentation European Association of Work and Organisational Psychology (EAWOP), 23 May 2015, Oslo.

Honneth, A. (1995). *The Struggle for Recognition. The Moral Grammar of Social Conflicts*. Cambridge: Polity Press.

Hua, W., Whitener, E.M., Maznevski, M.L., Sæbø, S.R. & Ekelund, B.Z. (2003). Testing the cultural boundaries of a model of trust: Subordinate-manager relationships in China, Norway and the United States. University of California, Los Angeles. UCLA International eScholarship Repository: http://repositories.cdlib.org/asia/eslictme/chntrans07/

Krogh, G. Von., Ichijo, K. & Nonaka, I. (2000). *Enabling Knowledge Creation: How to Unlock the Mystery of Tacit Knowledge and Release the Power of Innovation*. New York: Oxford University Press

Lane, H., Mendenhall, M., Maznevski, M.L. & McNett, J. (2004). *Handbook of Global Management. A Guide to Managing Complexity*. MA: Blackwell Publishing

Matoba, K. & Ekelund, B.Z. (2013). Diversity Icebreaker in the development of a third culture. *Sietar presentation in Mannheim*, 21 May. Presented in B.Z. Ekelund & P. Pluta, (2015). *Diversity Icebreaker II. Further Perspectives*. Oslo: Human Factors Publishing, pp. 62–103

Nordvik, H., Berg, A. & Ekelund, B.Z. (2000). 16PF5 development in Norway. *Journal of the Norwegian Psychological Association*, 31(5): 437–447

Pluta, P. (2015). Systematic use of humour in HR training concepts – an example of the Diversity Icebreaker. Paper presented at the 23rd Nordic Academy of Management Conference NFF 2015 – Business in Society, Copenhagen Business School, 12–14 August 2015

Rubel-Lifschitz, T., Arieli, S., Elster, A.Sagiv, L. & Ekelund, B.Z. (2014) Organizational intervention for increasing interpersonal interactions and creativity. The 7th Annual Euromed Academy of Business Conference. Kristiansand, Norway, 18 Sept 2014

Smith, P.B., Andersen, J.A., Ekelund, B.Z., Graversen, G. & Ropo, A. (2003). In search of Nordic management styles. *Scandinavian Journal of Management*, 19: 491–507

Thomas, D.C., Fitzsimmons, S.R., Ravlin, E.C., Au, K., Ekelund, B.Z. & Barzantny, C. (2010). Psychological contracts across cultures. Perceptions and responses to violations. *Organization Studies*, 31: 1437–1458

Watson, W., Kumar, K. & Michaelsen, L. (1993). Cultural diversity's impact on internal process and performance: Comparing homogeneous and diverse task groups . *Academy of Management Journal*, 36(3): 590–602

West, M.A. (2000). Reflexivity, revolution, and innovation in work teams. In: M. Beyerlein, D.A. Johnson & S.T. Beyerlein (Eds.), *Product Development Teams: Advances in Interdisciplinary Studies of Work Teams* (pp. 1–29). Stamford, CT: JAI Press.

Whitener, E.M.Brodt, S.E., Korsgaard, M.A. & Werner, J.M. (1998). Managers as initiators of trust: An exchange relationship framework for understanding managerial trustworthy behavior. *Academy of Management Review*, 23: 513–530

World Value Survey; http://www.worldvaluessurvey.org/wvs.jsp

Zander, L. (1997). License to lead. Dissertation for Stockholm School of Economics

10 Dignity and personal development

"You cannot expect people to do such things, unless they get paid." This was my father's way of making a conclusion, very often at the dinner table, when I asked the question "Why do people not…?" His answer provoked me. I did not want to think that women and men are rational self-interested transactional creatures. I wanted humanity to be contributing to goodness and beauty. I decided not to be cynical about human potential, and to show the world alternatives.

The positive bias of my experience

I have worked for more than 30 years as an organisational consultant with a core competence of a psychology education. Since I am a psychologist I have probably been approached by managers that were more than normally willing to communicate and reflect, open for change, humanistically oriented, and willing to invest in employees' personal growth and competence. They have been more than willing to invest in human capital. They have had time and money for a long term investment. They probably had an idea that involving people and trusting them will lead to employee empowerment, increased motivation, and willingness to devote energy and time to organisational goals. All of which I think is true, and which is the professional experience that has formed my practice. I am aware that my client experiences do not reflect what is most frequent among Norwegian leaders, but the experiences probably reflect a future oriented "Good"-oriented sample. For this reason, it is important to learn from these experiences. These are the examples that grasp the positive opportunities in the future.

Given that most of my cultural upbringing and business practice is in Norway, I assume that ideas and concepts developed here have an explicit and implicit cultural flavour. But, since Norway has been defined as an attractive place to be from a human values point of view, it might be of interest to look upon the experiences reflected in this book as potential ideas to be applied outside Scandinavia. For this reason, let me share with you at the end what is my cutting edge perspective on the use of Diversity Icebreaker in work life contexts; contexts where people are organised with economic exchanges in order to produce products and deliver services. But, now, back again to the economical perspective that is reflected in my father's comment.

Limitations of economic models

There is growing criticism of classical economic thinking these days. Some elements of the critique come from alternative economic models which in general are named "heterodox economic models" and includes, for example, evolutionary, feminist, post-Keynesian and ecological economy. There are different very promising initiatives. A student led initiative that began to be coordinated in Tübingen, Germany in 2012, and now all over the world, "Rethinking Economics" is a coordinated initiative to broaden the educational scope in teaching in economy at universities and business schools (http://www.rethinkeconomics.org/).

In the Academy of Management, the world largest management organisation, the "Alternative economic forum" was established in 2013 promoting a community perspective on economics. The Transdisciplinary Journal of the International Society for Ecological Economics states that "Ecological economics is an interdisciplinary field defined by a set of concrete problems or challenges related to governing economic activity in a way that promotes human well-being, sustainability, and justice" (https://www.journals.elsevier.com/ecological-economics/).

The Humanistic Management Network was established in Berlin in 2011 and defines itself as "an open and collaborative platform aiming to facilitate broad based progress towards a humanistic economic paradigm" (http://www.humanisticmanagement.org). Most of the critique towards classical economy is due to the negative effects of positioning profit maximisation or more precisely maximisation of shareholder's wealth as the one and only goal. Especially the short term economic reporting of the stock market where groups of volatile investors have financial outcomes as the only variable, are perceived as dysfunctional practices. In some periods, the major increase in GDP has been the growth in the financial industry where financial value is created by financial transactions, not in real material or service production. People earn money by moving money. There is only a limited added value for most people of having financial investors exchanging money in between their pockets. And, there is a large distance between these values created by money transactions and what is good for people and in terms of ecological sustainability.

Historically, businesses were mostly family owned with values of caring for people, society and the long term care of local resources. Owners usually invested their time and effort in their localplaces, and were not motivated by investing money just anywhere in the world in order to make the highest return on their investments.

A response to these negative effects of a one dimensional economic perspective has been the introduction of triple bottom line in the accounting of firms; financial, social and environmental, coined for the first time by John

Elkington (2002). The fourth quadruple bottom line denotes a future-oriented approach (future generations, intergenerational equity, etc.). It is a long-term outlook across generations that sets sustainable development and sustainability concerns as more important than short term social, environmental, and economic considerations (Waite, 2013).

In economics and in accounting practices, it seems as if the added dimensions are nice to have when the economic goals are achieved. The core business is still production and profit. Social, environmental and future oriented perspectives are secondary, things that are added in order to let the firm shine in a public sphere that is concerned with more than shareholders' wealth. The reason is that an organisation that cannot produce profit at the same level as its competitors will not survive. Money will be pulled out and salaries will not be paid. Profitability is roughly speaking an indication of good management of resources. And, nothing is won by bad management of resources.

The social, environmental and future oriented reporting by organisations might lead to economic side effects. A positive organisational image on these issues might be important for hiring the most talented people as well as making the organisation more attractive to customers. These elements are again important for long term profitability, thus also of interest for the shareholders' values. This is illustrated by the fact that introductions of more multifaceted modern management have been seen to have a direct effect on the firm's value at the stock market.

In my field of psychology, business oriented researchers at management schools seem to have accepted a research practice where productivity and efficiency are the main outcome variables. The researchers look for more human oriented managerial practices and document that they have a positive economic effect. Money rules even in our field of organisational psychology. There are few researchers that state that certain good practices are important only because they create positive results for the people involved. I think we have to raise this concern, especially when material over-production and poor waste management seem to be amongst the main causes for environmental disasters. We have to strengthen the value created for people in organisational processes and not only focus on the products being created.

I think it is time for us to position what is important for human beings at the centre of our activity and what is needed to take long term care of the natural world. Instead of seeking maximum economic results, we should use the word "economically" in its real meaning, as the careful way of managing our resources, whether the resources are material resources, money, people, or time. Being economical means taking care and utilising resources. It is important to not let money become the goal in itself.

Money is nothing more than a transactional instrument in the exchange of value between people. It is a means to make transactions between people easier. It is not an end goal in itself. If we position human needs and dreams in the centre, there are some things that money can buy – and there are some things that money cannot buy. There are some human needs and dreams that are not controlled by money.

My view is that we have not spelled this out clearly enough, how these needs and dreams can be satisfied inside work life organisations. I think we have to be more explicit about what values and practices in and between people satisfy true needs, what works for people and nature and what constitutes the beautiful world we all are striving for. This is a way of putting people at the centre. This is what humanistic management is about.

It is my strong belief that work life organisations today can become the place where human beings can develop being good people individually and collectively. And, I find no other places where adults can, in a more dedicated form, share such ideas and jointly improve the dignity of being a human being. In the traditional management field, the questions are: "What are our goals? How do we organise ourselves to achieve these goals?" If we apply the same elements and position putting, "being a good person and living a good life in the centre", the questions are: "What is the meaning of life? How do we live together to satisfy the meaning of life?" Then we are touching core elements in philosophy, religion, psychology and more.

We have to answer the basic questions and find answers together through communication and interaction. I have mentioned Axel Honneth's social philosophy of recognition. People need to be recognised which means they need to be heard, belong to a group, and contribute to something more than themselves (Honneth, 1995). Is this something that can be a good guideline for how we live and work together in work life organisations? My answer is very clear. The answer is YES.

In work life organisations we can ask such questions as "What is good for me? What is good for you? If acknowledgement is important, how can I act and communicate towards Others in order to value the Other? How can I talk and use words that make it attractive to continue communicating and to be included in the communicative and interactive practice?" These are questions that normally have been sequestered in academic disciplines in the humanities. In my view, we can position these questions in work life and then bring the questions, not the answers, out of the university context and into work life practices.

Values based management as a way of forming organisational culture

If we compare working life today with what was typical 50 years ago, the differences in the role of work are huge. Our parents went to work in order to finance their life. The jobs were often prescribed precisely and with a stability in function. They spent the money with the family outside the organisation of work. Today the meaning of work has expanded exponentially, not for all employees, but for those who are involved in self-managed jobs, managers and employees working with change. Increasingly, more organisations involve employees in everyday decision making, which also leads to a situation where the need for employee competences expands into fields of problem solving and social interaction.

The workplace invites employees to be involved, reflect, and develop themselves in order to fulfil their role. Personal development and training both for individual growth in social competence and ethics has gradually become an important part of everyday life in modern organisations. As an adult, it seems that modern organisations today give individuals possibilities of working with values and ethics more than local community, expanded family and religious congregations. Perhaps the working life is the place where decency and dignity both for individuals and collectives are most often in focus. Values based management then becomes an issue for "the meaning of life" and not only a smart tool to make workers produce more value for stakeholders and customers. Given this change in working life, the question is how can the Diversity Icebreaker concept contribute to increased focus on these human oriented values. Delegating responsibility and accountability to employees at all levels is one of the practices we see being stimulated with Diversity Icebreaker seminars. The case illustration below is an example of such an involvement across all levels in the organisation.

Case: Employeeship at Norwegian University of Science and Technology

In 2011–2013 Linn Slettum Bjerke were leading the employeeship (a word created to mirror leadership) program with all employees at technical and administrative functions at the Norwegian University of Science and Technology. The ideas behind employeeship are many, but a core element is the idea that all employees can decide for themselves how they can contribute in a way that takes into consideration the overall goals of the organisation and its leaders. In order to make this happen, the individual employee needs to see the connections between everyday activities and overall goals. In this developmental program all 400 employees were organised into 13 different groups that followed the same program in a nine month period. The first day was about "you and your communication" with Diversity Icebreaker and Red, Blue and Green. The second day was about the team and how to solve problems together. The third day was about how the whole team could work in practical terms in relation to the overall goals and important internal customers. In the end, the program culminated with a collective concert and celebration where each group presented a collective product of art; most examples were musical presentations. The evaluation by the leadership months after the program was that staff had an increased sense of collective identity and stronger commitment, evidenced by an increased willingness to be accountable, to act accountably, and remarkably there was reduced sick-leave.

An independent evaluation done by a psychology department concluded that the communication model (Red, Blue and Green) and the dedicated involvement from the leaders in supporting the program were important contributors to the program's success. Saksvik et al. say in their report:

> Many of those interviewed pointed at the Diversity Icebreaker and the processes around the test. One of the interviewed said: "What is important with such a test is that everyone uses the same type of language. It has given me a tool that I can use talking to anyone in the organisation."
>
> (Saksvik et al., 2015)

This case illustrates how a shared language like Red, Blue and Green can facilitate communication. In this case, the Diversity Icebreaker seminar involved all levels within the organisation. They worked together in the seminars and across different follow up tasks dependent on the level and types of responsibility. Shared language is a central component of organisational culture. The Diversity Icebreaker seminar, utilising Red, Blue and Green, seems easily adoptable in programs such as the one described here.

Diversity Icebreaker also has some explicit and implicit values. These values can be discussed, highlighted and applied integrated in values based management. One of the values that is most mentioned is "respect" for people with different predominant colour preferences. Not only respect in a passive form, but respect in a way that implies searching for an interaction where people find the best ways of contributing together to something larger.

In 2015, I was approached by leaders of an organisation who wanted to strengthen the collective commitment among employees. I was asked to initiate a process that could make everyday working life more attractive. In this case, I chose to focus both on the values that were common in between colours, as well as values that were unique for each of the colour preferences. In managing, it is important to balance focus on both these qualities. Shared values create cohesion, and unique values are the elements that acknowledge the individual in a diversified culture. You can see the process and the results described in this case study below.

Case: Villa Enerhaugen

Villa Enerhaugen has 65 employees with a huge variety of functions, competence and cultural backgrounds. They wanted to strengthen the collective commitment. We organised Diversity Icebreaker seminars and 12 mono coloured working groups, where we asked them to identify attractive values in the psychosocial area of work. They created numerous ideas of Red, Blue and Green values, which we summarised in Figure 10.1. The different workgroups then picked the values from this overview that were most relevant for their own working group. The shared model was the one that united the whole organisation.

Preferred ideas of work climate due to colours

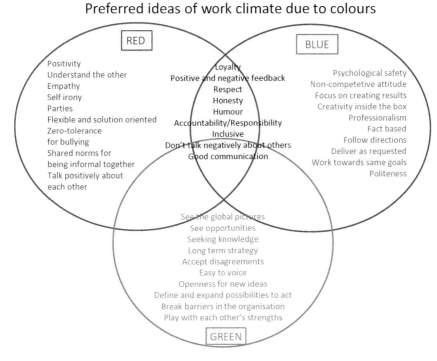

Figure 10.1 Preferred ideas of work climate due to colours

Cross-cultural conflicts at workplaces

In the case mentioned above, a large group of recent immigrants was involved. I have mentioned earlier that the challenges across cultures in relation to work related issues are huge and the case above is presented without identifying these issues of conflict. Of course conflicts will arise due to cultural differences. Also the process of resolving the conflict is not a process of finding solutions based on balanced conflict resolution processes (in the sense of between equals) where everyone has the same level of influence. We may talk as if these issues can be solved in a way that makes everyone happy because a more creative and better solution develops due to good communicative skills. This is not always true. There are some non-negotiables in all cultures that immigrants do not have the same advantages of winning over when conflicts emerge. This is especially so in relation to issues where local people have spent generations developing a societal practice that for them represents progress and modernity.

In the area of employee involvement, here in Norway, there has been a long and strong tradition of listening to employees in decision making. It is a cultural norm that decisions are made relevant for employees. It is even regulated by law that the leader must inform the employees, listen to their concerns and see if what they voice has implications for decisions or implementation. A leader who relies only on written information, and does not involve him/herself in direct consultative communication, will have problems implementing the decisions and lose legitimacy as a leader. This is something we treat as an important element in leadership training. In most other societies, you find employees with a huge respect for people with positional authority. In Norway, this is not a widely shared value among employees.

Similarly, in a management training session here in Norway, I was asked by a female leader in the cleaning industry what to do when men from the Balkans, working in subordinate roles, did not listen and communicate with her because she was a woman. From my point of view, this is not acceptable. It is not an issue for negotiation. In Norway we normally look upon such negative attitudes towards women as leaders as examples of old-fashioned ideas not in line with modern practice. As Edward Said stated: "When we look at people from other cultures, we will most likely see a 'lack of' the same level and quality as we think we represent ourselves" (Said, 1979). However, in order to have continuity in our own culture, we probably have to accept that a host country organisation and community has the right to adhere to some core non-negotiable values and ways of going about things. Even so, what is non-negotiable is probably something that can be discussed, acknowledged as a difference so as to diffuse unspoken tensions around it, but still not negotiated.

I guess most people will find it fair that the rights to influence the decisions are stronger for hosts versus in-comers or guests. The conflicts that emerge in these ways, are those conflicts that make everyone more aware of the cultural values that they themselves adhere to and hold as non-negotiable. The truth is that often when we ask people to write a list of those values that are absolutely non-negotiable under any unusual circumstances, the list is very short and focuses mostly on shared human rights to life, dignity and basic needs.

In Chapter 6 I presented the cultural dimensions that I find relevant in work life contexts. These dimensions can make it easier to be aware of the diversity of cultural values that might become a part of our work place discourse when immigrants express their values from their background. Rights for women and cultural practices for employee–leader relations are cultural artefacts that represent many generations of struggle to create a better world. Values, attitudes and practice develop gradually with a huge variety of different alignments in different subcultures. It is not realistic that this is something that can be easily and quickly changed due to ordinary information given in introductory courses to immigrants. If we have taken centuries, for instance, to have women as equals in the work place, governments, to vote, to head the church, then how long will it take, and how flexible are we in the change of attitudes and values in relation to immigrants? More than normal patience and tolerance is needed for them to integrate into the workplace while still maintaining their core identity. Some questions and discussions have to be started again to bring newcomers on board.

In the descriptions of cultural values, there are different methodological approaches. In the Globe study (House et al., 2004) respondents were asked to describe both what is espoused and aspired to around a certain value laden work life reality and their perception of what the actuality is, so that researchers could illustrate the gaps. If what is wanted is an illustration of dreams and ideals, then we can see normative statements in the data. And, across all countries it seems that most people in different countries want more participation, delegation, and a humane orientation, qualities that we normally see more frequently in northern European and Scandinavian work life. This indicates that our ideals are shared by many, and it legitimises a kind of non-relativistic attitude to many of these qualities. The desire and need to communicate and act with decency and respect in dialogues, discussions and debate, demonstrates acknowledging the Other in a way that makes people feel respected. This promotes change for all involved, a change process that is more urgently needed and more challenging at this point in time than what we have seen earlier in history.

Humanities in crisis

Over the last decade, the crisis of humanities has been a major topic in European universities. The reduction of resources for teaching and research in these areas is an important element in this crisis. The public debate has also involved people outside academic institutions. Globalisation, and increased cross-cultural interaction in particular, has reinforced the relevance of humanities towards a broader contribution of humanities in society. A special interest has been around the concept of "Bildung" that traditionally has been a personal project for the individual to develop capability to "think, grow and reflect" as a continual improvement to the ideal of being human.

On behalf of a Norwegian foundation Fritt Ord (Free Speech) Helge Jordheim and Tore Rem (2014) spent two years with a working group of experts to address the crisis in the humanities. They have pointed out that purely a continuation of traditional teaching and research inside classical disciplines of humanities at universities will have a limited contribution. They state that the universities' contribution, their contract with society, should be more aligned with the ideas of "Bildung". They stress the importance of moving from the individual to the collective "Bildung". They refer to Kant who states that "Bildung" can only develop in a public setting with others, in a project of deliberation from imposed norms. As such the "Bildung" becomes a political and collective process where individual consciousness and active citizenship are the goals (Nussbaum, 2016).

Jordheim and Rem also argue that the challenge today is to develop critical thinking and empathy in a way that makes citizens global beyond their embeddedness within their own national histories. Ecological challenges as well as other issues are challenges where national decisions have little effect and global solutions are needed. It is a huge question as to whether the ecological crisis will or should make it a necessity to accept global organisations' influence and authority beyond national interests.

How can Diversity Icebreaker be applied for complex, wicked and Grand global ecological challenges?

In the introduction of this book, I focused on how meeting Others was relevant for global challenges. I have further focused on three different types of diversities: personal qualities of Red, Blue and Green, interdisciplinary paradigms and cultural dimensions. I have explored some of the ecological challenges due to climate crisis, and large groups of immigrants where such differences are relevant. The case I present below comes from a research project addressing climate issues across many countries, disciplines and organisations.

Case: Cannes – a multidisciplinary and multinational research project

In 2013 an EU project was started with the ambition to study and develop measures of the effect of sulphur dioxide on buildings representing important cultural heritage. There were 58 representatives from 12 countries and 21 organisations involved. They had a kick-off meeting of three days. The representatives were recruited from very different positions and backgrounds: managers, biological experts, meteorologists, project coordinators, journalists, etc. They wanted a) a collective experience that was positive in a traditional kick-off format, b) an experience that could facilitate interaction between the participants across disciplines and status, and c) a concept that made it possible to talk about how to facilitate interactions between different types of diversities. Diversity Icebreaker was applied for this purpose. Anecdotally, when I was in Greece in Spring 2018, I saw the results in one of the castles that had an improved cultural heritage protection referring to the successful EU project.

Diversity Icebreaker has often been applied as an integral part of the kick-off of a project, especially when people do not know each other and come from very diversified backgrounds. The uncertainty of meeting Others is turned into a positive experience and a feeling of common ground. In projects like this, the individuals are recruited due to their individual competence, a competence that he/she very often does not share with the Others in the project. Their unique identity in the project is the reason they take part. Combined with what I have mentioned earlier around the importance of professional identity, it is easy to see that "I am not like you" is a frequent experience and topic of communication. In such projects it is important to create a common ground of positivity and trust before entering into the problem-solving stage where the different disciplines are identified as relevant to problem definition as well as problem solving.

Part of this common ground is a shared feeling of mastery, or being able to manage differences elegantly and productively. In a research interview with Mary Yoko Brannen, she formulated a sentence of learning. *"If I know nothing about China, but I know that the Chinese person I have in front of me is Blue, I know what to do. And, since I know that he knows I am Green, I expect him to have the same understanding of how to approach me."* She was reflecting on the individual's mastery.

When everyone in a group is involved in Diversity Icebreaker people witness their friends, colleagues and even newcomers also mastering this language and interaction. This collective belief that Others are also mastering this interaction leads the group into a collective feeling of mastery that makes it safe and easy to apply the categories of Red, Blue and Green.

The kick-off creates a starting point. Another example of a long term use of Red, Blue and Green in relation to the complexity of cross-cultural and interdisciplinary diversity is the master program in Agroecology at the Norwegian University of Life Sciences. This is an international program created by a group of researchers and teachers from different countries. Since 2000 they have organised a master program with about 25 partici-pants recruited globally, including (but mostly from) the USA, Germany, France, Italy, India and Norway. Each year around ten different nationalities are present in the class-room. They come from different scientific fields like agronomy, environmental studies, developmental studies, sociology, anthro-pology, politics and law. They have a one-week introductory preparation before they start experiential learning in groups with field work. Diversity Icebreaker has been used for the last ten years as part of this introduction and as a language for interaction and reflection. The program won the national educational quality prize in 2016. In their text for nomination they started by describing the challenge the way it is described in the case belown (Lieblein, 2016).

Case: Master Education in agroecology

Major challenges in education for sustainable development

> Sustainability challenges are highly complex with intertwined envir-onmental, economic, political, and social components. Attaining sustainable food production and consumption is a prime example. How can people and countries provide food for their growing populations in the context of climate change, increasing depen-dence on fossil fuels, an accelerating loss of biodiversity and qual-ity farmland, and a global shortage of fresh water? This inherent trans-disciplinarity of sustainable development poses new chal-lenges to educators. How do we design learning activities that will prepare future professionals with competencies to push the green shift to serve our rapidly changing society (Francis, 2011)?
>
> Knowledge about sustainability and development is essential but not sufficient for this large task, and new knowledge alone does not necessarily lead to responsible action. Education for sustainable development needs to address the large gap between knowledge and action by fostering competencies to overcome this disparity. Thus, the challenge is to design and implement an

effective learning strategy that enhances both the students'
understanding of complex situations and their individual and collective abilities and motivations to take responsible action.

(Lieblein, 2016)

A third example of the use of Diversity Icebreaker in relation to a complex
and climate related issue, outside universities and research projects, is the case of
the largest off-shore windmill project in the UK, in Scotland (Brynhildsvoll,
2019). In this project, the Diversity Icebreaker concept was applied in relation
to vendor–supplier selection and development. The Red, Blue and Green was
introduced in the assessment centres. Using these lenses, the quality of supplier's competence was assessed before a decision was made about which supplier
would win the contract. In the execution stage, the assessment and facilitation
of the quality of cooperation in the team processes, Red, Blue and Green was
applied as a feedback language from the behaviour consultants. This was perceived as a central component in the supply chain development and later on
integrated in the company's best practice for such large projects.

In these examples the Diversity Icebreaker has been applied in interdisciplinary and cross-cultural contexts. As such, they combine all the three
diversities that have been central in this book. Historically Red, Blue and
Green have been qualities where the main focus has been on the individual and
social interaction. In the interdisciplinary context we suggest that Red, Blue
and Green also can represent perspectives across disciplines (Ekelund & Moe,
2016). And we have started to involve major organisations in the political arena
of environmental politics to apply such a model.

There is of course a limit to how far value is added by using a simple model
of Red, Blue and Green when approaching wicked, complex and Grand
challenges. I invited a MENSA group in their annual meeting in 2015 to
explore how far such a model of simplicity could be applied when facing
complexity. Wisely, they said that the main strength of the model was the
social and communicative component which is a very important internal part of
complex problem solving, as well as in market communication and in public
communication where you want to reach out to most people. As recounted in
Chapter 2, Red, Blue and Green was created in 1995 in order to facilitate
communicating about energy conservation with the very diverse spread of
electricity users across a society.

In addition, the MENSA participants pointed out that some inter-disciplinary
perspectives and challenges could be organised using Red, Blue and Green as a
common structure. The mapping could have some commonalities that made
involvement and communication around complex and difficult issues easier. At
the same time, they assumed that in-depth analysis and execution of tasks needed
a much more disciplinary specific complex understanding. Indeed, this is the
classical balance between the importance of common ground for everyone being

involved and for what is a unique contribution from the individual. A classical dilemma in all diversity management.

Dignity triggered by Diversity Icebreaker

I hope it is clear that Diversity Icebreaker is an intervention that is often used to improve communication and interaction within an organisation. The goal has been to improve both efficiency, as well as increase creativity. But, as I have also mentioned, an important potential contribution is to build an inclusive organisation with positive norms and attractive values. The case study of Villa Enerhaugen is an illustration of how employees can identify important values that make being a member of the organisation attractive. These values might be identified at the last stage in the Diversity Icebreaker seminar where we ask "What can we learn from this experience?" There are some values that are suggested more often in such processes. Here are some examples of these values which I think can contribute to a collective understanding of a dignified community (Ekelund, 2018). All the values are about the management of diversity in people and perspectives and how this can be integrated in interactive processes.

Acknowledgement. It is important to acknowledge the Other. This implies respecting the right of each person to voice opinions, to be seen as a valuable member of a group, and to encompass qualities important for the greater good.

Complementarity. Participants suggest that people with different colours need each other. This holistic perspective is meant to integrate all three different perspectives. The Diversity Icebreaker concept integrates people as well as different perspectives on many different types of challenges.

Egalitarianism. In the workshop, participants say that none of the colours is more important than the others. This stands out as a contrast to most real life situations where power and expertise are unevenly distributed. The workshop can function as a mirror for a more open reflection about similarities, differences, justice, and functionality.

Multiple views. This stage raises the issue of "When we have different values and wishes, how do we solve such a situation in a way where everyone contributes? How do we move on in a way that shows respect of each other's value and values?" The ability to ask good questions and learn from others is an important competence. If we want democracy, everyone should act in a way that makes it possible for others to freely voice their opinion without fear of negative consequences. The social philosopher Benhabib (2011) has mentioned this quality as an ethical responsibility each of us have if we want to protect democracy. Self-reflection and playfulness with stereotypes, about oneself and others, without being punished, makes this seminar into a process where people talk more openly than they usually do. The collective reflection creates a collective cognitive closure when the diversity of values and talents are integrated in a synthesis across polarities or conflicting views.

Accountability. Participants take charge and start to talk about how to realise the potential within their diversity. This attitude of accountability maximises the possibility of finding a way of interacting to do just that.

Besides the norms and values that are included in the diversity perspectives, there are other qualities that also contribute to the attractive adoption of the language with Red, Blue and Green:

Positivity. The positivity in the seminar is experienced in many ways. First of all, with the starting point of the positive qualities of the colours. Being perceived as positive by Others makes being together more attractive. The joy of being with Others is very often the conclusion, both being with people that are similar, and with Others who are different, but with a functional and beautiful interplay of complementarity.

Trust. In the Diversity Icebreaker seminar, the norms about having a positive understanding of the Other and reciprocity in complementarity, set some expectations of being treated well. The collective understanding of how to make interaction work well, leads to a positive expectation about future processes. The norms about working well together lead to increased predictability. All these elements build trust.

Since the start of this book, I have focused very much upon the practice of asking questions like "What kind of norms and values do we want to have in our workplace?" I have illustrated some of the answers above. In my view, the practice of questioning is the critical thinking that is the focus of "Bildung" the way it is described by Jordheim and Rem (2014). The basic questions are "What are our goals? And how do we get there?" I have focused on how we as human beings develop ourselves through dialogue with Others, learning together as well as developing solutions together on these questions. I have illustrated some of the positive answers that often come out of such discussions. In a world that is very diversified, we might assume that the answers will be just as varied as the background of people being involved. Are there some common goals and norms that can bring us all together and unite us when we raise these questions?

Evelin Lindner created World Dignity University in 2013 (http://www.worlddignityuniversity.org/joo/), a virtual global university where humiliation and dignity are the core subjects. Her intention is to contribute to a world where dignity is the major rule for interaction. She refers to United Nations process after the Second World War where statements and words were sought that everyone in the world could agree upon. And the word dignity is the core they agreed to. The Universal Declaration of Human Rights is a milestone document in the history of human rights. It was drafted as a common standard of achievements for all peoples and all nations. It sets out, for the first time, fundamental human rights to be universally protected. The first sentence is: "Recognition of the inherent dignity and of the equal and inalienable rights of all members of the human family is the foundation of freedom, justice and peace in the world."

The concept of dignity is something that can be practiced in everyday interaction, and the explicit and implicit values and norms of the Diversity

Icebreaker seminar can be applied as a starting point for such discussions in different seminars and organisations. If living with dignity in practice is the goal, how can we achieve this in practice? My concern has been to contribute to such discussions at work places around the world, and, through that process of communication, develop values and practices that are more aligned with the real needs and dreams of human beings.

The Diversity Icebreaker seminar is a local communicative practice. Among social philosophers I have mentioned Alex Honneth (1995) as a person who has formulated answers that are meant to be true, good and beautiful as generalised statements. And, such answers can inspire us in our everyday search for a better practice. Another author that has focused on and elaborated on how dignity manifests in interaction is Donna Hicks (2011). She has made ten statements of what dignity is about. And, I want to finish this book by citing these statements as the last pieces of good advice.

Essential elements of dignity (reduced form)

1   Acceptance of identity: Give others the freedom to express their authentic selves without fear of being negatively judged.
2   Recognition: Validate others and be generous with praise.
3   Acknowledgement: Listen and respond to others' concerns.
4   Inclusion: Make others feel that they belong.
5   Safety: Make others feel safe, and not afraid of retribution due to their free speech.
6   Fairness: Treat people justly, with equality.
7   Independence: Empower people to act on their own behalf.
8   Understanding: Make others experience that what they say matters; active listening.
9   Benefit of the doubt: Start with the other as a person who acts with good intentions and integrity.
10   Accountability. Take responsibility for your actions, apologise when doing wrong, and commit yourself to change hurtful behaviour.

"As long as communication goes on, life is worth living." This sentence is a constant reminder of the value of communication for human beings. In my contact with philosophers, they attribute this statement to Ludwig Wittgenstein. I want to rephrase this and state "As long as good/dignified communication goes on, life is worth living."

Bibliography

Benhabib, S. (2011). *Dignity in Adversity. Human Rights in Troubled Times*. Cambridge, MA: Polity Press
Brynhildsvoll, I. (2019). *Prinsipper for bedre innkjøp*. Oslo: Fagbokforlaget
Ekelund, B.Z. (2018). *Diversity Icebreaker and Leadership*. Oslo: Human Factors

Ekelund, B.Z. & Moe, T. (2016). *Innovation Booklet*. Oslo: Human Factors

Elkington, J. (2002). *The Sustainability Advantage: Seven Business Case Benefits of a Triple Bottom Line*. Gabriola Island, BC: New Society

Francis, C.A., Jordan, N., Porter, P., Breland, T.A., Lieblein, G., Salomonsson, L., Sriskandarajah, N., Wiedenhoeft, M., DeHaan, R., Braden, I. & Langer, V. (2011). Innovative education in agroecology: Experiential learning for a sustainable agriculture. *Critical Reviews in Plant Sciences*, 30(1–2 Special Issue): 226–237

Hicks, D. (2011). *Dignity. The Essential Role it Plays in Resolving Conflict*. New Haven, CT: Yale University Press

Honneth, A. (1995). *The Struggle for Recognition. The Moral Grammar of Social Conflicts*. Cambridge: Polity Press

House, R.J., Hanges, P., Javidan, M., Dorfman, P.W. & Gupta, V. (2004). *Leadership and Organisations: A 62 Nation GLOBE Study*. Thousand Oaks, CA: Sage

Humanistic Management. http://www.humanisticmanagement.org. 30 Nov. 2018

International Society for Ecological Economics. https://www.journals.elsevier.com/ecological-economics/. 30 Nov. 2018

Jordheim, H. & Rem, T. (2014). Hva skal vi med humaniora?Oslo: Stiftelsen Fritt

Lieblein, G. (2016). Nomination for Active Learning Model, applied for NOKUTs award for teaching.

Lieblein, G., Breland, T.A., Østergård, E., Salomonsson, L. & Francis, C.A. (2007). Educational perspectives in agroecology. Steps to a dual learning ladder toward responsible action. *NACTA Journal*, March: 37–44

Nussbaum, M.C. (2016). *Not for Profit. Why Democracy Needs the Humanities*. New Jersey: Princeton University Press

Rethinking Economics. http://www.rethinkeconomics.org/. 30 Nov. 2018

Said, E.W. (1979). *Orientalism*. New York: Vintage Books

Saksvik, P. Ø., Olaniyan, O. S., Lysklett, K., Lien, M. & Bjerke, L. (2015). A process evaluation of a salutogenic intervention. *Scandinavian Psychologist*, 2, e8.

Waite, M. (2013). SURF. Framework for a sustainable economy. *Journal of Management and Sustainability*, 3(4): 25–40

World Dignity University. http://www.worlddignityuniversity.org/joo/. 30 Nov. 2018

Also by the author

Books

Ekelund, B.Z. & Jørstad, K. (2002). *Team Climate Inventory – Intervention Manual* (Danish). Copenhagen: Danish Psychological Publication

Ekelund, B.Z. & Langvik, E. (Eds.) (2008). *Diversity Icebreaker: How to Manage Diversity Processes*. Oslo: Human Factors Publishing

Ekelund, B.Z. & Pluta, P. (Eds.) (2015). *Diversity Icebreaker II. Further Perspectives*. Oslo: Human Factors Publishing

Training material

Ekelund, B.Z. (2018). *Diversity Icebreaker and Leadership*. Oslo: Human Factors Publishing (Norwegian and English)

Ekelund, B.Z. & Moe, T. (2016). *Diversity Icebreaker. Innovation*. Oslo: Human Factors Publishing (Norwegian and English)

Ekelund, B.Z. & Rydningen, M. (2008). *Diversity Icebreaker: Personal Workbook*. Oslo: Human Factors Publishing (Translated into 6 languages)

Articles and book chapters

Ekelund, B.Z. (2009). Managing diversity in teams (Norwegian). In Fyhn, H., *Kreativ tverrfaglighet, teori og praksis*. Oslo: Tapir forlag, pp. 182–205

Ekelund, B.Z. (2010). Diversity Icebreaker in conflict management. *EFPSA Journal/ summer school documentation*

Ekelund, B.Z. & Moe, T. (2014). Team leadership in community childcare (Norwegian). In Kvello, Ø. and Moe, T., *Barnevernsledelse*. Oslo: Gyldendal

Ekelund, B.Z. & Pluta, P. (2013). Diversity Icebreaker: Training of flexible diversity management. In Witkowski, S.A. and Stor, M. (Eds.), *Sukces w zarządzaniu kadrami. Elastyczność w zarządzaniu kapitałem ludzkim. Tom 2.Problemy zarządczo-psychologiczne* (Vol. 2, pp. 273–280). Wrocław: Wydawnictwo Uniwersytetu Ekonomicznego we Wrocławiu

International conference presentations

Israel Organizational Behavior Conference, 3 Jan. 2018. Tel-Aviv, Israel: Arieli, S., Rubel-Lifshitz, T., Elster, A., Sagiv, L. & Ekelund, B.Z., Psychological safety, group diversity and creativity

Nordic Intercultural Communication, Conference, 23 Nov. 2017. Jyväskylä, Finland. Ekelund, B.Z. & Pluta, P., Reframing Others in Colors of Mastery

Academy of Management, 8 Aug. 2017, Atlanta. USA. Ekelund, B.Z., Nordic perspectives on humanistic management

"Inspiring Learning Life". Conference, 13 April 2016, Sundvolden, Norway. Ekelund, B.Z. & Steier, F., University of South Florida. From dialogue to trialogue: Promoting systemic learning and innovation

African Academy of Management, 8 Jan. 2016. Nairobi, Kenya. Canney Davison, S., Ekelund, B.Z., Gjerde, S., Boodhun, V., Guttormsgard, I., Malde, Y.S., Handeland, A., Dahlmann, O.P., Gyan, K.A., Dybwad, A., Johnston, K., Fjell, K. & Lane, H., Trainer experiences applying Diversity Icebreaker in 15 African countries

Academy of Management, 8 Aug. 2015, Vancouver. Professional Development Workshop. Vinkenburg, C.J., Ekelund, B.Z. and Romani, L., Writing (and talking) differently about diversity: Addressing the normalization of othering

European Association of Work and Organisational Psychology (EAWOP), 23 May 2015, Oslo, Norway. Symposium. Ekelund, B.Z., Moe, T., Ekelund, S.M. and Winje, T., A language perspective of Diversity Icebreaker

The 7th Annual Euromed Academy of Business Conference. Kristiansand, Norway, 18 Sept 2014. Rubel-Lifschitz, T., Arieli, S., Elster, A., Sagiv, L. & Ekelund, B. Z., Organizational intervention for increasing interpersonal interactions and creativity

SIETAR (Society for Intercultural Education, Training and Research) Europe. Tallinn, 20 Sept 2013. Ekelund, B.Z., Diversity Icebreaker applied in conflict management from Norway, through the Balkans to the Middle East

Democracy and Diversity in Higher Education. Buskerud University College, 13 March 2013. Rossi, A., Van Egmond, M., Orgeret, K., Pluta, P. & Ekelund, B.Z., Promoting democratic practice through 'Diversity Icebreaker' in multicultural student groups

16th International Workshop on Team working (IWOT), Trondheim, 6 Sept 2012. Ekelund, B.Z., Post-postmodern perspectives on Scandinavian teamwork practice. Lessons from playing with different paradigms

SIETAR (Society for Intercultural Education, Training and Research). Europe conference, Krakow, 23 Sept 2011. Ekelund, B.Z., Mokastet Pemzec, A.B. & Crestani, M.A., Diversity Icebreaker in international contexts

Academy of Management Annual Meeting, San Antonio, Texas. 12 August 2011. Ekelund, B.Z., Rossi, A.L. & von Egmond, M.Use of Diversity Icebreaker and learning styles in multicultural teaching settings. Professional Development Workshop

International Association for Cross-Cultural Psychology, Istanbul, Turkey. 2 July 2011. Ekelund, B.Z., Rossi, A.L. & von Egmond, M., Use of Diversity Icebreaker and learning styles in multicultural teaching settings

ACM International Conference on Intercultural Collaboration, 19 Aug. 2010, Copenhagen, Denmark. Invited Key Note Speech: Diversity Icebreaker in international communication

ECER (European Educational Research Association). Helsinki, Finland. 26 Aug. 2010. Ekelund, B.Z., Rossi, A.L. & von Egmond, M.Use of Diversity Icebreaker and learning styles in multicultural teaching settings

58th Annual Conference of the Serbian Psychological Association, Zlator, Serbia. May 2010. Ekelund, B.Z., The descriptive, functional and beautiful qualities of Diversity Icebreaker. Research challenges in three different perspectives

South Eastern European Regional Psychology Conference, 1 Nov. 2009. Sofia, Bulgaria. Ekelund, B.Z., Davcheva, L. & Iversen, J.V., Diversity Icebreaker: Developing shared understanding of cooperation

Dialogin. The Delta International Academy Conference. 18 Sept 2009, York, UK. Ekelund, B.Z., Social construction of interpersonal categories

The 11th European Congress of Psychology, 10 July 2009. Oslo, Norway. Ekelund, B. Z., Diversity Icebreaker: An individual psychological test applied for collective reflection and deliberative dialogs in groups and organizations

SIOP: Society for Industrial and Organizational Psychology, 4 April 2009. New Orleans, USA, Rothausen, T.J. & Ekelund, B.Z., Construct validity and comparison of two psychological type models. Diversity Icebreaker compared with MBTI

Academy of Management Annual Conference, 9 Aug. 2008. California, USA. Ekelund, B.Z. & Maznevski, M.L., Diversity Training: Are we on the right track?

Academy of International Business, 3–5 July 2008. Milan, Italy. Ekelund, B.Z., Shneor, R. & Gehrke, B., Diversity Icebreaker in cross-cultural training

Academy of Management Annual Conference, 7 Aug. 2007. Philadelphia, USA. Ekelund, B.Z., Diversity Icebreaker: Social construction of team roles as a tool for managing diversity

Global Forum, IGB Consortium. 21 Feb. 2007. Tokyo, Japan. Ekelund, B.Z., Diversity management in multinational companies

IWOT: 10th International Workshop on Team Working. Trondheim, Norway. Langvik, E. & Ekelund, B.Z.2006. Managing diversity: How to heterogenize teams in order to create self- and team knowledge

SIETAR (Society for Intercultural Training and Research) Conference. London, UK. 9 Sept 2006. Ekelund, B.Z., Team roles as Diversity Icebreaker

Academy of Management Annual Conference, Atlanta, USA, 13 Aug. 2006. Ekelund, B.Z., Diversity Icebreaker applied in International Management teaching

Index

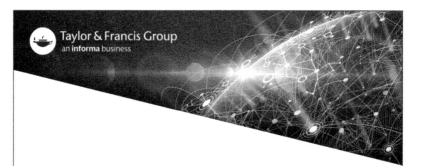